CW01650251

BLAZING GLORY: THE PRETENDERS

Dedication

To wise boys and girls who are ready to love Jesus and live prepared for his return.

Blazing Glory

The Pretenders

Karen Davies

Illustrated by David Colbourne

CROSSED OVER

Copyright © Karen Anne Davies 2010

The right of Karen Anne Davies to be identified as author of this work has been asserted by her in accordance with the Copyright, Designs and Patents Act 1988.

First published 2010

Published by Crossed Over
www.crossed-over.org

ISBN: 978-0-9559463-2-5

All rights reserved.
No part of this publication may be reproduced or transmitted in any form or by any means, electronic or mechanical, including photocopy, recording, or any information storage and retrieval system, without permission in writing from the publisher.

Biblical quotations are taken from *International Children's Bible,* New Century Version: copyright © 1983, 1988 by Thomas Nelson Publishing Inc. Anglicised edition: copyright © 2008 Authentic Media.

Illustrations by David Colbourne
Edited by Anna Leggett

Book design for the publisher by Biting Back Ltd
Printed in Great Britain by CPI – Cox & Wyman, Reading

Contents

Symbols in *The Pretenders*

As you read the story you will discover four powerful symbols. Use them as keys to unlock the amazing mysteries that are hidden between the pages of this book.

1. When you see the magnifying glass, it's time to stop and look up important messages in your Bible. Open your Bible at the place shown and read what Father God has to say. (See "The Bookworm's Guide to the Bible" on page ix to find out how to navigate your way around the Bible.)

2. The feather is a very important symbol and is only given to those who are good listeners. It points you to special words in the Bible. As you read these words, hear the gentle voice of Father God speaking especially to you. (See "The Bookworm's Guide to the Bible" on page ix to help you find the Bible passages.)

3. Whenever you see this symbol, pray to Jesus along with the characters in the story. To pray just means to talk to Jesus, as you would talk to your best friend. Your prayers will unlock the help that you need.

4. This symbol represents the Olive Grove. Spend friendship times alone with Jesus in this special, quiet place. Here you can enjoy talking to Jesus in  prayer and listening to his voice through the words in your Bible. The more you do this, the more valuable oil you will have to light your own lamp to show you the way to Blazing Glory.

The Bookworm's Guide to the Bible – The Living Manual

Hey, here's a little guidance so you can wriggle your way through the pages of your exciting Bible. Follow these simple steps and dig away. When you see the  and  symbols in the story, here's what to do:

↘ The Bible is made up of 66 books. There are 39 in the Old Testament and 27 in the New Testament.

↙ There are two Contents pages in your Bible which will help you to find the page number each book is found on. Look at the Old Testament Contents page just before page 1 of your Bible for books in the Old Testament, and the New Testament Contents page on page 1108 of your Bible for books in the New Testament.

- ↖ Every book has chapters.
- ↗ The next step is to find the correct chapter number. It's the largest number on the page.
- ↙ When you have found the right book and correct chapter you are just seconds away from the verse.
- ↙ The verses are numbered in every chapter, with little numbers right next to the words you are to read.

For your first dig, why not look up and read 2 Timothy chapter 3 verse 16. If you can't find it, don't worry. Why not ask someone who can show you how to find it? Think about what it says here – how Father God, the author of the Bible, inspired men to write down what he wanted to say to his people. The Bible is God's living message to the world.

Character Photo Gallery

The Preps

The Pretenders

The Stalkers

THE ROBOTS

Sardines

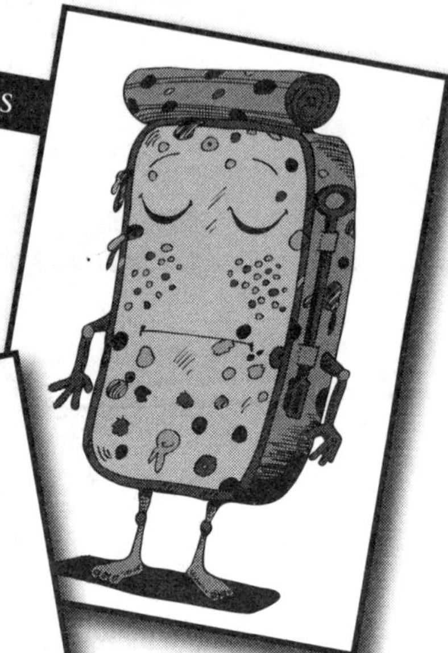

Deli

Epee

THE ROBOTS

I-Spy

Mums

Od

THE ROBOTS

Rara

1
Anti-Freeze

Who could have dreamt that watching birds would turn out to be this exciting? It's time to wake up because this tale isn't just a dream – our feathered friends come with a true message from Blazing Glory. An important new day is about to dawn, so listen with your ears and watch with your eyes wide open. This true story is mixed with imagination, fun and peril.

As keen-eyed birdwatchers, follow the colourful trail and you will learn the difference between what is true and what is fake. This will be no ordinary journey but one where the trail will grow brighter and brighter each day. By the time you have finished, you will have discovered a great event that is about to take place. So, be prepared as you watch for the morning and wait for the Master, Jesus, to return.

Oscar the eagle flew high above the clouds, carrying his two friends Penny the sparrow and Melody the songbird on his long, strong back. These young Glides were ready for a lifetime of adventure, following the way to Blazing Glory. Melody took in the breathtaking view while plugged into her iPod, listening to her favourite rock music. The loud music took her mind off how high they were flying and helped her

to overcome her fear of heights. Penny sat comfortably on Oscar's back, cleaning her wings by licking her wing feathers. She loved the view, but even more she loved the bright fruit badges that decorated her plain brown wings. She had earned these on their first *Trick or Treat?* adventure. Oscar, being a fine young student, had learned to trust Father God for everything and so was able to rest on the wind thermals which carried them high into the clear blue sky.

It seemed like they were being carried into the perfect day. Melody started to tap sharply with her claws on Oscar's wing as she listened to her favourite bird tunes. A nail on one of her claws caught on the edge of Oscar's fruit badge of patience. It chipped Melody's bright-pink nail polish which annoyed her no end. Melody gave a tug with her claw which started to fray the stitching on Oscar's badge. This ruffled Oscar's feathers but he reminded himself how important it is to continue doing the things taught in his manual, the Bible, so he didn't get cross. Being like Father God was a lesson to put into practice every day of his young life. The fruit badges had been awarded to remind the Glides of this truth.

Despite the commotion on board the flight, Oscar felt turbulence in the wind. The gentle breeze had changed into swirling currents coming from every direction. The four winds – North, South, East and West – were all blowing at the same time. Lots of other birds came flying in from every angle. This great gathering of birds began to blacken the sky. Penny became a little afraid and she clung on to Oscar for reassurance. Stuck in this traffic jam of migrating birds, Oscar had no option but to go with the flow and follow the growing crowd of feathered friends.

Beneath the giant flock of birds lay fields rolling into the distance like a perfect picture. The fields were coloured with yellow buttercups and wild red poppies. The flowers swayed in the breeze as the four winds beat across the landscape. Which way should they go? The force of the winds took control as the birds soared like freedom flyers towards the morning sun.

There was an unfamiliar sight in the distance. Tall metal pylons surged out of the ground like a line of robots defending the land. One by one, the birds found a pylon platform to rest on. As far as the eye could see there were birds resting on the pylons and the long wires joining them together. The birds seemed to be watching and waiting for something special to take place.

Oscar found a platform for himself and his two passengers and gasped in wonder at this increasingly amazing sight. Penny caught a floating feather in her beak. It carried words from Father God on it. She got out her Bible and read the message to find out what they should do.

Psalm 130 verses 5 & 6

No sooner had she finished reading the words to Oscar and Melody than Devine the dove gracefully flew in, carried by the morning winds. He perched beside them. Devine is the promised Holy Spirit who is sent by Father God. He teaches and guides friends of the Master, Jesus, along the road of truth that leads to the heavenly kingdom of Blazing Glory.

Devine the dove was electrified with light. Every bird watched this spectacular sight and there was a stunned silence. He commanded such awesome respect from the gathering of birds. With a loud penetrating voice Devine spoke to the flock of birds.

"Watchmen, watchmen . . . wait for the dawn!"

The birds were puzzled by these strange words and waited to hear further instructions. Devine explained to them that this was the Last Hour before the return of the Master, Jesus.

He challenged the birds to be like night watchmen and to wait for their Master. He then firmly warned them to be properly prepared for this hour – not a normal hour of 60 minutes, but rather a short, unknown amount of time. After the time had passed, things would change forever. During this short waiting time they were to train and get prepared so that they would not fall away and lose their way to Blazing Glory. He asked them all to follow him on this 'Last Hour' adventure so that they could become members of the 'Preps'. This was the name given to the group of followers who were prepared and ready for the Master's return.

Melody had been a little distracted with her iPod while Devine had been talking. The battery was beginning to run flat. She found a connection on the pylon to plug it into to recharge.

"I think I will stay here and work on my gift of singing," piped up Melody. "Besides, the battery on my iPod will not last for a long journey. He did mention a long journey, didn't he? I'm really not sure I want to go."

"Are you sure you don't want to go?" replied caring Penny. "Devine said there wasn't much time left before the Master's return." She was a bit concerned that their special Glide group, the group of friends who had got together on the 'Trick or Treat?' adventure, was breaking up.

"Look, there are other songbirds who are going to fly around here and work in these fields for the Master. You never know, I may be able to do a music tour to some local festivals and sing to others about Jesus," responded Melody, swinging her black feathers to the beat of her music.

"Well, as long as you are sure you are doing the right thing," Oscar responded. "We will try and come back this way once the mission is complete, if there is time. But you need to be sure."

"Oh, I'm sure I'll be alright," said Melody, a little bit more hesitantly.

Devine rose up. He began to hand out small magnifying glasses to anyone prepared to go on this Last Hour quest. Devine deliberately called the mission the 'Last Hour quest' to alert the birds to the urgency of the task.

"The days ahead are going to be difficult. Sometimes it may be hard for you to understand what is happening," warned Devine very clearly. "Use your magnifying glass to read your Bible. It will make every word stand out. It will make the Master's instructions clear. The Master's words in the Bible are there to help you find the right way to go."

When Devine had given each freedom flyer a magnifying glass to go with their Bible, he gave them the following verse to look up. The magnifying glass magnified the words and everyone reading them understood what they meant.

Psalm 138 verse 2

In choosing to show them this verse, it was clear that Devine was preparing the freedom flyers to focus on Jesus and his words above everything else.

As Devine hovered over them, something very peculiar began to take place. A dark, thick mist began to creep all over the ground. Everywhere the birds looked, the mist was crawling over and covering the whole landscape. Fortunately, the birds were all high above the ground so they weren't touched by the mist. The mist looked like anti-freeze spray and as it spread it put to sleep all the life in the fields. It paralysed the swaying flowers and caused everything living on the ground to be still. Curiously, as the mist moved across the ground, the image of the evil vulture Vermont became visible in the dark swirls.

Without a moment to spare, Devine spread out his huge wings and flapped his feathers. The strong breeze he created kept the watching birds awake. He then gave them some strict instructions. He told the birds they must keep to the same flight position above ground and not drop below it. This would help them to avoid the mist and to remain in heavenly places near to the Master, Jesus. Devine then told them to read the following Bible verse with their magnifying glasses:

Ephesians chapter 1 verse 3

"These words are telling you that you will remain safe if you maintain your flight position and stay close to Jesus," explained Devine. "Be careful because the mist will rest on the earth for all of this Last Hour. Those who come under its influence will turn against Jesus, the Master. They will fight against him," he warned in a serious tone. "You are all Preps now because you are being called out and made ready for the Master's return which will be very soon. From now on you will live free and blessed but remember that dangerous and perilous times are ahead. Your most important task is to be on the lookout as you  pray for the strength to keep going towards Blazing Glory."

In a flash of blinding light, Devine took off to lead the group. As he spread out his strong wings in the sky, a crack of lightning lit up the heavens. The birds could see that the mist had covered over the trail on the ground. Thunder rolled across the skies as if Father God was creating a flight path for the birds to follow.

Oscar and Penny said a quick, tearful goodbye to their friend Melody. They embraced her with strong wing-hugs. With no time to lose, Penny then jumped up onto Oscar's back. She safely tucked her magnifying glass inside her Bible and put them into her flight bag. Oscar didn't need to flap his wings but just held them outstretched as he rose up on the powerful slipstream that had been created by Devine's enormous wings. They surged miles across the land, keeping a safe distance above the creeping mist. Devine continued to lead the way as they flew high over the small, sleepy towns below. A strong, walled city lit up the distant horizon. Lights in the small houses twinkled in the mist. Taking a sharp right turn, Devine flew around the outside of the city wall and set the course straight ahead to a tall mountain.

"Get ready for touchdown on Mount Olivet," Devine called back to the following birds.

He touched down gently on the strong mountain. One by one, the birds landed and then flocked forwards in their hundreds, responding to Devine's call to become Preps.

Oscar and Penny hovered around in the sky for a while, looking for a space to land near Devine. Devine caught sight of them, and remembering these special birds from their previous travels, he made room for them by his side. Oscar gently glided in, and landed with barely a ripple. Devine smiled lovingly at them both. He remarked how much Penny had grown as he made space for them under his caring wing.

"You are young, but don't let anyone treat you as if you are not important. I will take good care of you both," he smiled.

They both thought at the same time that Devine was such a kind friend and guide. Oscar tried to impress Devine with a tale or two, desperately trying to show off his gift of knowledge. Devine listened patiently. He had given Oscar this gift on their previous journey from the Camp of Life Academy and he was not impressed that Oscar was now showing off. However, what did gain Devine's attention was the fraying thread on Oscar's badge of patience. It had started to come away from his wing feathers. Devine was worried that the badge would fall off his wing, so he gave Oscar a verse to read from the Bible while he secured the thread back onto his badge.

The verse was one they had learned on their graduation day from the Camp of Life Academy:

Revelation chapter 3 verse 11

"Remember, you must keep following the things I've taught you," said Devine. "You've started flying well but you must continue and finish well too."

Oscar and Penny paused for a moment with Devine and thought about how important the fruit badges were. They knew that if they continued to apply the qualities they represented (truth, humility, justice, love, joy, peace, patience, kindness, goodness, faithfulness, gentleness and self-control) in every situation, then more good fruit would continue to grow in their lives. Good fruit is a reward from the Master in Blazing Glory, and friends of Jesus who have lots of it show that they are like him in the way that they serve others.

The huge flock of Preps relaxed at the top of great Mount Olivet. From there, they could see hundreds of olive trees at the base of the tall, mysterious mountain. They knew, thankfully, that they were safe from the dark, creeping mist resting on the city below. Devine asked all the Preps to rest where they were for the night and to take it in turns to be on watch until the morning. He arranged to meet them early in the morning in the Olive Grove at the base of the mountain and instructed them not to be late.

Penny was missing Melody but then soon realised she had the whole of Oscar's belly to herself as a nice feathery double-nest. Oscar, ever keen to learn, decided to be a watchman and could barely contain his excitement. While Penny snuggled into his cosy feathers, he would watch and wait for the morning. He knew that one day soon his Master would return to this mountain. This thought made him warm and happy inside.

2
Morning Watch

The sun stretched its first ray over the mist in the city, like a strong arm pushing back the fast-disappearing night sky. Oscar jumped up quickly, forgetting that Penny was asleep on his belly. She tumbled to the ground and rolled like a penny coin down the mountain.

"Aghhh, ouch, help!" cried Penny as she rolled at a frantic pace.

Oscar chased after Penny but she had raced into the Olive Grove before he could get to her. Battered and a bit bruised, Penny wondered where she was. Oscar came flapping through the olive trees. He then slipped on the trail of oil that ran from the trees' branches. Like grease lightning, the two friends came crashing together. They landed in a heap, looked sheepishly at each other and began to giggle. Devine, who was awake and waiting for the Prep students, flew over to the noisy pair of feathered friends. Oscar and Penny tried to stand up to attention when they saw Devine but they just kept on slipping over with oily joy.

"Do days always start like this in the Olive Grove?" asked twittering Penny, unable to stand still.

"Wherever I am, there is always joy!" exclaimed Devine,

who couldn't resist joining in on the moment. "The morning watch is a very important part of the life of all Preps. Use your magnifying glasses and read the following verse from your Bibles. You will see there that you will find strength in my joy for the whole day!" sang Devine, smiling, as Oscar found the right page with his sticky wings and Penny giggled the words out loud.

Psalm 16 verse 11

Oscar, ever watchful, noticed the oil pouring from the surrounding olive trees and seeping all over the lush green grass. It looked like a long, oily beard. As the grass moved, it tickled his claws and edged his wing feathers with splashes of oil. Oscar chuckled away to himself. Penny hopped over to see what was so funny and had a 'tweetment' of oil herself. With one hop too many, she fell over and rolled with delight in the oily grass. Penny shone with oil and happiness.

Devine wondered what he was going to do with his happy young Preps, given the frenzied start to the day. Oscar tried to pull himself together with a long, deep breath, and combed down his feathers with the oil so that he looked a bit more respectable. It gave him a very set but styled new look which he actually quite liked! He gave himself an intelligent centre parting in the fringe of feathers on his head and then asked Devine what the oil was for.

"The oil sets you apart for the Master's service. If you have lots of oil, it shows others that you have spent time with Jesus, the Master, by reading your Bible and praying. It also helps you to use the gifts and skills you have been given by Jesus in the right way," taught Devine.

Oscar and Penny were beginning to understand how important it was to spend lots of friendship times alone with Jesus in the Olive Grove. They both enjoyed talking to Jesus in prayer and listening to his voice through the words in their Bibles.

"The oil is also needed for fuel in your lamps. Having a lamp full of oil allows you to shine the Master's words of light onto every situation you face, and it also lets you lead others along the right way. This is especially important for this Last Hour. At the moment, the dark creeping mist makes it difficult to see the right way to go. Your lamp must be filled with oil every day so that it does not run out. And, if the Master returns at night, you must have oil so that you can see him coming," warned Devine.

The young Preps were a little puzzled. Devine took Oscar

and Penny over to a special olive tree to continue their lesson. The roots of the tree seemed to be marked and stained with small drops of red blood. Oscar and Penny wondered what had happened here. Devine got out his magnifying glass and Bible and read out the following verses to explain the situation to the Preps:

Matthew chapter 26 verses 36 to 46

"We are now standing in the very place where Jesus spent his last hour on this earth. He was here with his disciples before he died on the cross for the sins of the whole world," said Devine, a little disturbed. "He had asked his friends, the disciples, to watch and pray for just one hour because he knew what was about to take place. Sadly, the disciples were tired and fell asleep in the garden. The same instruction given to the disciples is for you too, young Preps, if you are going to be ready for the Last Hour before the Master returns. You must watch and pray so that you are not tempted to fall asleep under the effects of the menacing mist," warned Devine.

Oscar and Penny gasped in horror at the tale, wondering if they were ready to be Preps.

"How can I stay awake all the time?" sighed Penny. "And does this mean I can never go to bed in my comfy nest?" she yawned. Little Penny needed plenty of sleep.

Devine smiled as he tried to help the young Preps understand. He wasn't saying they mustn't go to sleep for a good night's rest. What he meant was that if they didn't watch and pray by reading their Bibles in the Olive Grove each day, then they would not think about the

Master's return. This would make them lazy in their work for the Master, helping others to see the way to Blazing Glory. They were being asked to stay awake in their understanding. A Prep must live prepared for the return of Jesus, the Master.

"You must be prepared even if you are young. If you do not watch and pray, then the mist will take you by surprise and you won't be ready for the Master's coming," remarked Devine most insistently.

Devine then showed the two Preps something they had never noticed before. He showed them that there were little, hidden pockets on their fruit badges. Inside these little pockets were tiny tube pots. These would contain the oil. The tube pots could be filled up with oil every day to help them on their adventures. Devine told them to remember the morning watch and to come to the Olive Grove daily to fill their tube pots with oil.

By now there was a noticeable noise coming from within the Olive Grove. Many other birds had begun to flock in. Devine waited for the latecomers to arrive and went over the things he had just explained to Oscar and Penny. Oscar and Penny were able to hear the same message again, so they now had a double portion of oil for the day! They were soaked in oil. Each little pot spilled over and the oil ran down their wing feathers and onto the ground.

All the Preps were now ready for their training. Devine led the flock of birds out of the garden and flew with strength and confidence around the side of Mount Olivet and out to a deserted valley. The sun was hot and fierce, but the oil, like a liquid shield, seemed to protect the birds from its harmful rays.

Down below, they saw a signpost pointing to a place

called Dry Valley, the name given to the area by the local birds. It was a dry place and nothing much grew there. All along the trail were metal bones and dry, rusty, metal panels. As the birds flew down the valley, the metal bones and panels began to rattle, making scary sound effects that gave a creepy atmosphere to the whole valley. Devine told the Preps to stay in formation and keep together because Dry Valley was a danger zone.

"Watchmen! Watchmen!" repeated Devine, over and over again. He could not allow the Master's followers to forget the importance of this flight. They had to keep watching and praying without stopping.

Dry Valley was one of Vermont the vulture's favourite battlegrounds. In the dry heat, Vermont and his vile assistants, the Stalkers, would wait like predators for any weary Preps passing through or passing out in the valley. This dark group of bandits was the greatest enemy of the Preps. Stopping students from finding the way to Blazing Glory was their first priority, and they would also battle tirelessly to trap any birds who had escaped the effects of the menacing mist while out on mission for the Master.

The Preps knew that they had to be really alert and keep to high ground if they were going to survive. They followed Devine sharply past the crack squad of buzzards perched on the dry branches of the parched trees that overhung the valley. At the highest point in the ravine, Devine landed with his large flock of students. He struck the rock under his claws with his sharp beak, like a match, and water came gushing out like a stream. All the birds drank from its supply as it flowed in a torrent, making pools in the crevices of the rocky ground. Oscar and Penny were allowed to drink from their own special pool. They were the youngest students to fly on mission that day.

"This trail we're on, the so-called 'narrow way', isn't easy," thought Oscar, as he slurped the cool, refreshing drink. But he knew it would all be worth it on the day when they would eventually see the Master.

Once all the birds had satisfied their thirst, they looked up. They could see in the far distance Prince Beelzebub, Vermont's right-hand vulture. The prince was dark and very mean. He was drilling his crack squad of buzzards as they hovered over the valley. They began to dive-bomb into the valley like missiles and pick up dry metal bones and rusty panels which they carried far off into the distance.

"Now, listen carefully," said Devine, starting the Preps' first training session for the day. "What I am about to tell you is very important. Vermont's cunning plan is to destroy the Master's worldwide Church of followers here on earth. The global Church is made up of lots of individual churches, in other words, gatherings of people who believe in Jesus. They usually meet in a church building. Vermont wants to stop people from making Jesus their Master, and make him their master instead."

The Preps all gasped and looked frightened. Oscar and Penny shook in terror as they remembered the trouble they had faced from nasty Vermont and his Stalkers during their *Trick or Treat?* adventures. Vermont and his followers were certainly up to their wicked ways again.

Devine continued to explain the situation. "Jesus's true followers are also called 'the body of Christ'. Let's all get our magnifying glasses and Bibles out and read about them in the following verses:

1 Corinthians chapter 12 verses 12 to 31

Can you see, now, exactly how those who make up the body of Christ here on this earth should behave together?"

The Preps all nodded. The passage in their Bibles painted a beautiful picture of how all of Jesus's followers should be working together.

"The problem is," continued Devine, "that Vermont and his cruel Stalkers are trying to mess everything up.

"How can they possibly do this?" shrieked Penny.

"I'll explain how. In each church building, there is a boiler room containing a robot. The robot acts like a mirror and reflects what is in the hearts of the church members. In a 'good' church, where there are pure hearts that follow the Master, all the robot's body parts are in the correct place, and the robot is programmed to work in the right way. So, when the power that drives the robot comes from Jesus, it will influence those who go to the church in a good way. In other words, a good robot programme will follow the instructions found in the Bible."

Oscar, who understood how robots work, got excited and tried to help with his playful knowledge. "Robots are not living beings but they can certainly influence those who spend time with them." He then began to act his age by walking around with jerky actions, pretending to be a robot. All the Preps were amused by his acting skills.

"That's right," smiled Devine, who then took off and plunged rapidly into the eerie mist in the valley in an attempt to gain the attention of the happy Preps. To their horror, he disappeared into the swirling mist. As he vanished, they noticed the images of the Stalkers in the dark swirls. The swirls were like claws trying to grasp hold of Devine. As the Preps huddled together, unsure of what would happen next, Devine emerged carrying lots of rusty metal bones and panels clutched firmly in his claws. Without spending any more time in the menacing mist, he landed firmly next to Oscar and Penny, dropping the robot bits and pieces in front of his students.

"What have you found, Devine? Just look at all the rust on the metal panels," commented watchful Oscar.

"Don't touch the rust, it's very dangerous," warned Devine. "I'm showing you these decaying things to help you understand Vermont's cunning plan. He has set up a scrap yard of metal robot body parts just to the north of the valley. Hidden inside the scrap yard is his Gift Factory. There he is very busy making faulty robots with faulty body parts. These robots are powered by Vermont himself and they are bad."

Oscar beamed with sheer delight. He was not paying attention and instead continued with his robotic actions. Devine gave him a stern look when he saw him smile because this was a very grave matter. Oscar immediately put on his most serious and studious face.

"There is nothing Vermont will not do to stop anyone from preparing for the Master's return," Devine carried on. "He has stationed himself in this Last Hour in Dry Valley and he orders the buzzards to steal all the dry metal bones and old rusty panels and then uses them to make his wonky robots, with faulty body parts that don't work correctly. He and his followers, who are called 'the Pretenders', then trick their way into a church building, sneak into the boiler room, and switch the good robot body parts for the bad ones. Wherever this happens, the Master's followers in that church begin to behave in a wrong way. They become manipulated and influenced by the wonky robot."

Penny raised her tiny wing because she wanted to ask Devine a question. All the grown-up Preps turned and looked at little Penny who began to blush.

"Yes, Penny," said Devine, "do you have a problem?"

She coughed and then spoke. "Can you explain a bit more about what a 'Pretender' is?" The grown-up Preps were wondering about this too, but were not brave enough to ask.

"The Pretenders come from the Gift Factory. They look and talk like real followers of Jesus but they are fake. Jesus calls them 'hypocrites'," answered Devine.

All the Preps gasped when they heard Devine use this word. From reading their Bibles they knew how much Jesus disapproved of any follower being a hypocrite. The Preps understood that to express their love for Jesus they must obey all his commands because actions speak louder than words.

Devine's eyes blazed with light as he looked at the group and continued to answer Penny's question. "Pretenders will sneak into a church and head for the boiler room to dismantle the good body parts on the robot and replace them with wonky bits. They then stay in the church, pretending to be real church members, but actually they are a bad influence. Watch out for them. They help Vermont with his plans without even knowing what they are doing. As a Prep, it is very important that you are trained to recognise a Pretender. They may look the part and say all the right things, but if their actions do not match their words then they are a Pretender."

The young birds were excited about the task ahead of them but they had just taken in so much information that their heads were spinning. They were worried that they wouldn't be able to remember everything Devine had just told them.

"Don't be alarmed," Devine reassured them. "Just remember that you Preps need to be watchful and always pray. You mustn't be influenced by the things around you, especially any wonky robots or Pretenders. You should follow and be guided by what you read in your Bibles. Jesus said that he will build his Church, and not even Vermont and his evil followers will succeed against it. Vermont lost the battle before he even started to fight!"

The Preps all breathed out huge sighs of relief. In fact, Oscar's sigh was so big that little Penny was blown over by the strong gust of his breath. "I didn't think playing and working with robots could be such a dangerous game," declared Oscar.

Devine laughed and then he prayed with the Preps. He asked them to come back to Dry Valley the next day, when an extraordinary event would take place. As the Preps took off, the oil in their tiny tube pots began to burn like bright lights. This helped them to see the way as they flew under the cover of light into the Olive Grove at the foot of Mount Olivet. Oscar and Penny volunteered for the first birdwatch that night, and all the Preps waited eagerly for the morning.

3
Dry Metal Bones

Oscar, being wise and prepared, decided that he and Penny should perch for the night watch in the highest tree they could find in the Olive Grove, high above the creeping mist that swirled over the ground. Oscar kept his glasses on as he watched and prayed. Unfortunately, it wasn't long before his eyelids became like lead weights. They were soon tightly closed, with his crooked glasses perched on the edge of his beak.

His 40 winks came to an abrupt end when a choir of songbirds decided to practise welcoming in the morning. Their little lungs were full of praise as they sang to Father God, their Creator. The olive trees began to sway, their branches looking like arms outstretched in worship. This meant only one thing. The arms of the tree no longer held Oscar and Penny, who dropped branch by branch to the ground with a 'plonk'.

Even though it was a shock to their feathers, the oily sap from the trees coated their wings as they fell. The smooth, shiny layer of oil made them ready for the challenges of the day's mission that lay ahead. The two young Preps were shaken and stirred as they recovered in a happy daze of delight. Since they were awake, they decided to make good use of the extra time, filling their tube pots with oil and spending time praying and reading over the previous day's Bible verses about the body of Christ, the Master's real Church. As they were young, they were used to doing their homework! They were happy to work hard because they knew it would pay off one day when they were put to the test.

After a light breakfast of figs, the two young Preps headed off to Dry Valley for the early morning meeting with Devine. It was still the early morning watch. The airwaves seemed clear of any of Vermont's vile assistants. The Preps flew through the valley unnoticed. The Stalkers always preferred to be out late at night which meant they would be up late in the morning. The early birds, Oscar and Penny, went to the highest point in Dry Valley and waited for the other Preps to arrive.

Devine was already waiting for them. There was a glow around him and a sense of wonderment could be felt in the breeze. The air was charged with excitement. Once all the Preps had assembled, Devine led a secret search flight around the valley amongst the dry metal bones. Oscar, with Penny holding tightly onto his back, flew as close as he could to the ground without touching the eerie mist. The mist, which seemed to find its natural resting place in low valleys, had poisoned Dry Valley, and everything there looked dead and lifeless. There were mounds of metal bones lining the valley and they were all very, very dry. Some of the metal joints had started to rust. After they had circled the valley a few times, Devine led the Preps back to the top of the hill. The mood of the birds seemed sombre. There appeared to be no hope of life in Dry Valley.

"Look at all the scrap metal bones," said Devine, sadly. "These were once healthy bones belonging to fine robots inside church boiler rooms, showing that the churches were full of energy and life and that Jesus's friends were following him correctly. In the past, many good robots came along here to Dry Valley to try to help the rusting robots that had got stuck in this dry place."

At this point, Penny began to check that the tiny joints on her small sparrow body were all working correctly. She looked carefully for any signs of rust. The little sparrow then began a keep fit exercise, touching her claws with her beak. Devine noticed that this was distracting the other students and so pulled her in close under his wing. She felt safe now, ready for the next alarming piece of news.

"Sadly, they didn't sense the danger they were in. Due to the large amount of menacing mist present here, they came under constant pressure to give in to Vermont and the Stalkers, and many of them did," explained Devine. "As a result, the members of the churches where the robots belonged, started to misbehave or leave, so the churches became lifeless and died too. The Master has sent me to help the perishing robots and to change them from being rusty to clean, polished and smooth-running. This will then give back life and hope to the churches they belong in. Jesus is not coming back for a lifeless Church that has given up but one that is healthy, beautiful and ready for his return."

Devine spread out his wings and began to speak words of life over the rusting metal bones in the valley. He breathed in a large lungful of air so that his bright-white chest expanded. He paused for a moment and then breathed out a long-lasting breath. It was like a strong, rushing wind that

whistled around the valley. The sound bounced off the hillsides as the rocks began to rumble.

While the ground grumbled and groaned, Devine explained to Oscar and Penny what he was doing and what was beginning to take place before their very eyes. "Through my words, the Master is bringing life and hope to all those who are watching and waiting for him to come again. What you are about to see is a picture of this life in action. Jesus's words bring life and help to the hopeless. Jesus is going to come back to earth soon, so now he is waking creation and all his friends so that they will be ready, watching and waiting for his return," said Devine.

The wind brushed through the feathers of the watching birds. Then there was a long, stunned silence. Suddenly the ground began to shake beneath their claws. All the Preps stayed as still as statues, not daring to breathe a word. Suddenly, the rusty metal bones in the valley began to rattle and clatter loudly, and the noise echoed around the valley. The sound bounced off the rugged slopes of the hills, creating a terrifying sound. No-one fully understood what was happening but they gazed with amazement at this incredible event.

Vermont and the buzzards became afraid. Wildly and loudly, they flapped their wings as they fled from the trees at the base of the valley and went into hiding. It was a strange and awesome sight. To the amazement of the Preps, the mist slowly began to lift from the valley as the buzzards left. This cleared the air space to reveal a very unusual sight.

Oscar and Penny moved in close to Devine, telling him they felt privileged to be part of this unique day. "Hmm," thought Devine as he hugged them with his strong caring wings, "or could that really be that they are a little scared?!"

As they looked more closely, Penny began to rub her little sparrow eyes. "Wow, look at how each metal bone is joining together. It's amazing! The metal bones and panels look like different sorts of robots," she squealed.

"I like the really tall, skinny, blue robot the best of all," remarked Oscar. "But it's funny how none of the robots can move."

Immediately, Devine lifted up his strong wings and flew swiftly around Dry Valley, pouring oil onto the joints of the stationary robots, and then landed back beside the watching Preps.

"Cor, I can't believe my eyes!" said Oscar as he straightened up his glasses. "All the rust on the metal bones and panels has disappeared."

"Amazing! Just look how shiny and polished they have become," remarked Penny as they both paused, expecting something else to happen.

"Why aren't they moving?" Oscar asked Devine.

Devine instructed the Preps to read out loud these important verses in their Bibles, which told a real bone-like tale:

Ezekiel chapter 37 verses 1 to 10

After these words had been spoken, Devine blew hard across the valley with tornado-like breath. Amazingly, life came into the shaking metal bones. What happened next could not be explained. A huge army of robots stood to their feet and began to march out of Dry Valley. All the Preps clapped as they watched this spectacular event. They had never seen anything like this before and they would never see anything like it ever again. All the robots marched in line like soldiers who knew their rank.

While the Preps talked excitedly amongst themselves, wise Oscar remained watching with his sharp eagle eyes. In the distance he saw Vermont working with Prince Beelzebub, calling his troop of buzzards back together. They did not waste a single minute regrouping because they knew time was short. As they advanced, the mist could be seen in their trail.

Oscar called out to Penny to come and take a look. "Quickly Penny, come and see what is happening over there!" shrieked Oscar as Penny zoomed over to see the strange sight.

"Aghhh, oh no!" cried the little sparrow in a frenzied flap. "They are going to attack the robots!"

She shrieked in horror, which brought Devine flying to their aid. From the high peak of the mountain, they watched Vermont's movements. From there, they saw how the buzzards swooped down and tried to pick off some of the advancing army of robots. Cruelly, they captured seven robots in their sharp claws and carried them away towards Vermont's scrap yard. What would happen to them at his Gift Factory was anyone's guess. Two of the robots struggled tirelessly with the enemies. They wriggled around bravely and managed to fall from the grip of the buzzards. All of a sudden, they fell and nose-dived rapidly to the ground inside the woods below.

Devine stood firmly, unshaken by what he had seen. Calmly, he turned to speak to the watching Preps who had gathered around Oscar and Penny. "All Preps are to work and train with the great army of robots that has marched out of Dry Valley. These fine repaired robots will be going out to station themselves in the boiler rooms of good churches in every part of the world, where friends of the Master will meet together. In these good churches, the Master's friends will be working properly together to spread the Good News about Jesus to those around them," explained Devine.

The Preps began to rustle their wings in excitement, ready to become part of the advancing army.

Devine paused and waited for their full attention before he carried on. With everyone on full alert, he continued. "It is important that the robots move to where I ask them to go. Each robot must go and station itself in the boiler room of a church near an Olive Grove. It is very important that, every day, the friends who go to that church find a good supply of oil. The oil is found by spending times of friendship with the Master, Jesus. The oil will produce light and can be used to prevent any rust damage forming on the robot. Your job," Devine continued, repeating some important instructions to the Preps, "is to pray and be awake when Jesus returns. Don't forget that to stay watching and awake you must spend time every day with the Master in an Olive Grove. Every one of you must find oil to fuel your own light of friendship with Jesus. Be warned that in this Last Hour, a great darkness will cover the earth. Vermont will work to try and prevent the Master's friends from watching for his return. You must pray to stay away from the slumbering effects of his menacing mist. You must also watch out for any Pretenders in the churches."

The huge flock of Preps rapidly took off in response to

Devine's command. There were thousands of birds of all different colours, sizes and species. Each one flew with guts and determination. As they flew, they formed into smaller groups, each small group then following a different robot.

The two youngest Preps stood still with their beaks wide open. They were amazed, afraid and speechless all at the same time.

Devine noticed their bewildered looks and then turned to speak with Oscar and Penny. Kindly he said, "You have done so well, my young friends, listening to and watching these very grown-up things. Even though you are not very old, you too must be ready for the Master to return. If you are ready to fly like eagles, you can come with me. I will take you on a life-changing journey. It will be a dream flight of weighty imagination," said Devine.

"We would love to fly with you wherever you are going," replied the two young Preps, beginning to wonder if they were just dreaming.

Why Devine had chosen these two young birds they could not imagine! First, he took them up to a high ledge. Their tiny claws grasped onto the narrow edge as he told them all about the ledge. This was his special Imagination Station. He told them how it is better to put faith into practice from high positions, in order to see things from God's point of view. "If you trust Father God and don't limit him, then you will be amazed at all the things he will do through you," said Devine with great excitement.

"But we are the least important birds in the group," said Penny, still trembling from the remarkable sights earlier in the day.

"There is one thing you must do. You can find out what this is in the following Bible verse," continued Devine. They carefully read the verse together and gazed at the skyline of opportunity that lay in front of them.

Psalm 2 verse 8

"Jesus came to save everyone, from all backgrounds and all nations, and to make them his friends. If you ask him, he will show you how you too can be part of this quest to help people to know and follow him," concluded Devine.

"That sounds easy. Even *I* can ask," chuckled excited Penny. Suddenly, her words were silenced by a loud knocking noise. "What's that rattling sound I can hear?" Penny asked, thinking it was the sound of more robots coming to life.

It wasn't the sound of rattling metal bones in Dry Valley – it was Oscar's knees! They were still knocking from watching the startling robot show. He tried to be big and brave just like little Penny but the shocking events were still affecting him. Devine placed his strong wing around Oscar and gradually the knocking stopped. Oscar felt calmed by the peace of being under Devine's wing.

"Our mission is to go and see what help is needed by the seven robots that have been captured by the buzzards," announced Devine. "We need to find the churches they have been carried off to and track down each robot inside each building. It is likely that we won't find the robots in the boiler rooms as I'm pretty certain the buzzards will have hidden them somewhere else, so we will need to be very alert and work quickly to find out where they are hiding and then try to identify what the problems are. This is a very important job for us to do because when Jesus comes back again, he will present his worldwide Church to Father God in Blazing Glory, and it must be pure and not have any faults," said Devine most firmly.

Oscar and Penny's eyes shone with the thrill of the task ahead of them. However, before the information had had time to sink in, Devine sighed and began to speak again.

"Before you get too excited about the thought of mending the robots and changing the churches, there is something you should know. We will only be able to spot the problems, we won't actually be able to fix the robots and make the repairs required to bring about the behaviour changes needed in the church members."

"Why ever not?" quizzed Oscar, sounding a bit put out. "Isn't it a waste of time, just diagnosing the robots' problems if we never know whether anything will change for the better?"

Devine paused to think and then continued. "Well," he said, "it's a good and a bad thing. Father God, because he loves those he has created so much, has given them freedom to choose. He can do all he can to help his creatures, but it is up to individuals to want to change and to improve their behaviour. This is where the second part of our mission comes in. We are to deliver a letter from Blazing Glory to each of the seven churches we visit. These letters, from Father God, congratulate the church members in each church for the things they are doing right, and warn them about the things they are doing wrong."

The young Preps gulped and jumped at the same time. They couldn't believe they had been selected to help Devine with this second very important task, too.

"So, you see," concluded Devine, "it's essential that we play our part in trying to identify problems, and in warning others to change, but the leaders and followers in the churches have to make the decision to change themselves. And we probably won't know whether or not that happens until the day the Master returns, when only those who are prepared, pure and ready will be accepted into Blazing Glory."

The young Preps had a big challenge ahead of them. They flew back to the Olive Grove with Devine so that they could rest there for the night. Devine settled his young students down in a special dove-feathered nest in the branches of an olive tree. They needed to sleep but first they read the following important verses in their Bibles, which helped them to understand the events they had seen earlier in the day:

Hebrews 12 verses 25 to 29

Wise Oscar talked with Penny about these verses long into the night. Their views on life and God had been shaken that day. This shaking had a positive effect because it helped them to understand Father God better.

"Isn't it strange how Father God is both so gentle and so powerful at the same time?" mused young Penny.

Oscar and Penny stretched out their wings and gave long yawns. As they settled down, they both seemed to grown an extra centimetre as they thought about how they were becoming more prepared for whatever Jesus wanted them to do.

4
The Gift Factory

The chilly night in the Olive Grove seemed too short for Oscar but too long for Penny. During the night, Penny was very fidgety. The cold night air made her keep pulling Oscar's wing, like a big feathered blanket, over herself to keep warm. As you can imagine, this irritated Oscar, so he didn't sleep very well. Penny, on the other hand, found great warmth and comfort under Oscar's long feathers so she was up, very loud and chirpy, at the crack of dawn. Yes, even before the songbirds! Oscar most certainly needed a little more sleep and his unhappy beak told a thousand stories. He was very grumpy. Happy little Penny tried to cheer him up with a joke.

"Why does a flamingo lift up one leg?" laughed Penny.

Oscar was too moody to answer, so Penny cracked the joke.

"Because if it lifted both legs, it would fall over!"

Penny squealed with sheer delight at her own joke but Oscar was certainly not amused and folded his wings in a huff. He tilted his head back and pointed his beak into the air in disgust. By this time, the  Olive Grove had become rather crowded with more birds wanting to become Preps.

This annoyed Oscar as the noise of chirpy birds got under his feathers and was giving him a headache. By the time Devine arrived in the Olive Grove, Oscar had developed a bad attitude. Oscar tried to find a quiet corner to sulk in.

Penny took no notice of him as she was more preoccupied with the colourful stripes that shone like a rainbow from Devine's wings. The colours became more and more vibrant as the oil from the olive trees soaked into his wing feathers.

"What are those eight colourful 'tick' stripes on your wings, Devine?" asked Penny.

"They are the 'Be-attitudes' found in Blazing Glory," responded Devine. "They represent what your attitude should be like as you journey to the heavenly city."

"Striking," chuckled Penny, who would give anything to improve the plain brown feathers on her wings.

Looking sternly but caringly at Oscar, Devine thought about how to deal with this difficult start to the day. He flew with Penny over to Oscar and smiled to cheer him up. "Let's go somewhere quiet for breakfast. I know a secret part of this Olive Grove that will help Oscar leave behind his bad attitude," suggested quick-thinking Devine.

They followed the blazing trail to the north side of Mount Olivet to an undisturbed pathway lined with fig trees. The leaves on the fig trees were the most vibrant green colour that Oscar and Penny had ever seen. Devine swooped down and picked a portion of ripe figs with his beak. Carrying the figs in his long claws, he then flew the young Preps to a peaceful terrace overlooking the desert landscape. After they had landed, they gave thanks to Father God for the food and then tucked into the healthy but sticky fruit for breakfast.

"The fact that these figs are ripe shows us that there is a

change in the season. This is one of the signs Jesus told his followers about, to help them watch and be ready for his return," explained Devine.

As the Preps chewed on the figs, Devine opened his Bible. It was an amusing picture as the figs had made his beak sticky and had caused the pages to glue to his beak. The friends worked together to scramble to find the correct page. It was a very funny, gummy lesson. Together they looked through their magnifying glasses at the enlarged words:

Matthew chapter 24 verses 32 & 33

"The earth is making itself ready for the Master's return, and so Jesus's friends should be doing the same thing," taught Devine. "The Master warns you to watch and pray as you see around you the changing signs that are written about in the Bible."

Feeling soothed by Devine's words and a good fun breakfast, Oscar finally began to talk and drop his bad attitude. He was now ready to pick up good attitudes and earn the rainbow stripes for his wings.

Devine continued. "Jesus taught his disciples how Father God expected them to behave. He always helped them with this, especially when they found it difficult. One day, as the disciples struggled with their attitudes, he took them to a mountain and gave them a lesson on how to be good Christians. He gave them a sort of code of conduct for how to live as a Christian, which you too should follow. If you live like this, then you will be good examples and you will be given happy Be-attitude stripes to wear."

He told them to look up the following verses in their Bibles, which showed them how to live as Jesus wanted them to:

Matthew chapter 5 verses 3 to 10

"These eight Be-attitudes will make you happy and cause a rainbow of promise to mark your wings with eight colourful stripes. The stripes will grow brighter as your behaviour towards the needs of others becomes better," said Devine. "As we continue on our journey together, you will see how powerful these attitudes can be in changing the world around you."

Oscar said the prayer for the day as he wanted to say sorry for his bad start to the morning. Then they all sat quietly for a few moments and watched as something unusual began to take place in the distant skies.

"Look over there!" gasped Penny. "What is that thick black puff of smoke coming from inside the woodland?"

"Hmm," replied Devine. "That is where the secret Gift Factory is located. Vermont must be very busy today. His factory pollutes the air as he makes wonky body parts out of the metal bones and panels stolen from Dry Valley. It is this polluting smoke that forms the menacing mist that creeps over the earth," warned Devine.

"Can we go and take a look and try to stop his nasty plan?" asked brave Oscar.

"His plans will not succeed," replied Devine. "He knows he has already lost the fight against Father God's kingdom. Vermont just wants to make as much trouble as possible before the Master returns to banish him and his wicked followers forever into a lake of fire!" continued Devine, getting a bit hot under his feathers. "It would be a good part of your training programme," he added, "to go and see

Vermont's phony plans. We can do this before we start trying to find the seven robots that Vermont captured from Dry Valley. Studying his plans will help you learn to spot what is fake, so that instead you will be able to identify what is true."

"Yippee!" shouted Oscar, who relished the idea of spying on Vermont's fake, flaky plans.

"Boo hoo!" cried Penny, who was not quite as confident as Oscar in becoming a spy.

"This test will help you to use the gift that Father God gave you, Penny," said Devine, reassuringly. "If you are going to serve like a true Prep, you must be able to tell the difference between right and wrong. You need to learn how to read the signs around you in this Last Hour, to be able to survive."

Without wasting a moment, Devine took off to lead the secret flight mission to the Gift Factory. Penny hopped up onto Oscar's back and then they locked into Devine's slipstream like a supersonic war plane. By staying on the secret winds, they remained invisible to Vermont's agents who were unable to detect any flights through the air space on their radar system. Flying full steam ahead, Devine led the Preps over Dry Valley. The high flyers flew fearlessly through the thick wood of dark, haunting trees and into the back yard of the Gift Factory.

The structure of the factory building looked like the shape of a robot, which puzzled the Preps as they stared in wonderment at this peculiar sight. The sheets of iron which held the body of the robot building together had been sprayed black. This was Vermont's favourite colour. The two windows in the top of the roof, which looked like a robot's head, were glowing with a red flashing light. Oddly, they looked as if they were working like eyes as they watched the grounds like an infrared camera. There were two other skylights on the robot's head. These were positioned on either side of the roof and looked like ears. One of the ears was flapping in the wind as it had been left open. The tap, tapping sound echoed around the back yard. Solar panels lined the front of the robot's head and snarled like sharp teeth at the Preps.

"What a big mouth the robot has," whispered fearless Penny.

Suddenly, Oscar and Penny jumped as the robot building rumbled and poured out swirls of menacing mist from the two small holes in the roof that worked like nostrils. Devine stretched out his wings and pulled the birds in close to his side. They knew they would be safe, sheltered under his wings.

The back yard was full of all kinds of smelly rubbish. Lots of big black rats scurried around the waste left on the ground. Oscar licked his lips because eagles enjoy eating a good juicy rat or two. Penny shuddered with horror as the rats were bigger than her and she quickly decided to become a vegetarian for the day! Firmly, Devine called for their full attention as he did not want his young Preps to be spotted and to come under attack from the Stalkers. He could see one of the Stalkers, Cyril the sulky snake, sliding around the overflowing bins behind the Gift Factory.

Oscar's attention was caught by a bright-red skip which looked like a mini red robot. It had a nasty, big, jagged mouth that liked to eat rubbish. The mouth was sharp so that it could chew all the unwanted stolen metal bones that were of no use to Vermont. The Night Wolf, the most dangerous Stalker, was busy sizing up some of the wasted body parts that had been thrown into the bright-red mini robot. He always liked to carry some of the spare parts on him so that he could trick his way into churches and exchange good robot parts for faulty robot parts in order to make the church members behave badly.

"He's the chief Pretender and a master of disguise," warned Devine, watching the Night Wolf's every crafty move.

Devine took off and led the Preps through the small, slightly open window on the side of the robot's head. The window led to the factory store room. To their amazement, it was like a treasure trove of gifts and expensive jewellery. The tatty exterior of the building disguised the undercover project that was taking place inside the factory walls. A dazzling glow bounced around the room as they stared at the finest-looking gold medallions. In the near silence, ticking watches shimmered on the cluttered shelves and work benches. Work was going on at a fast and furious pace inside the factory workshop. The stolen metal body parts, which had come from Dry Valley, were being formed into wonky robots. The Preps could see first-hand how Vermont would use these wonky robots to trick and then train the members of the Master's Church how to become Pretenders.

Looking as cunning as ever, Vermont perched in the robot's head on the rafters inside the Gift Factory. He was smirking with great pleasure as he knew that if these wonky robots looked a bit like real robots then he could trick Preps into believing that it's OK to work together in a wrong way. Vermont, an expert in fraud, would use all the shiny gifts to distract the Preps, hoping they would sell out and become Pretenders. He would do this by placing greater importance on the shiny gifts than on obeying what is found in the Bible. Then they wouldn't notice that the wonky robots were not working properly.

"All that glitters is not gold!" roared Vermont at the top of his lungs, enjoying his cunning, deceitful plan. This made the Preps shudder with fright.

The robots that were being assembled looked weird. Some

of the robots had one big eye and a huge mouth, while other robots had too many ears. One robot was slumped in the corner because it had lost its head.

"Look at that funny-looking robot over there," whispered Oscar as they peered down onto the factory floor. "It has arms that are really legs and there are no toes on its feet!"

"What's going on?" asked Penny. "And what's the loud noise screaming in my ears?" she whispered as she tried to plug up her tiny ears with the ends of her wings.

"That's the sound of the Pretenders. Pretenders move about in a very noisy way because they have no oil. Rust starts to form on them and on the wonky robots because they don't get oiled. A Pretender will claim to follow the Master but will rarely spend time in the Olive Grove. With little or no personal Bible reading and prayer, their oil supply quickly runs out. Pretenders don't mind making squeaky noises from being rusty because, just like Vermont the vulture, they are always trying to bring attention onto themselves. However, rust only forms on the insides of Pretenders, so it's hard to spot them. The First Commandment in the Bible is to worship only Father God, but Pretenders worship Vermont and themselves. As a Prep, you should always put Father God first in your life, and you should offer any praise you receive to him, rather than keeping it for yourself to make you feel important. Be careful of Vermont because he is a con-artist and all his work is fake. Before he turned bad, he used to live in Blazing Glory but he started loving himself and not God, and his trickery caused him to fall from Blazing Glory."

A loud bell suddenly sounded in the factory as Vermont's workers were given a short break for lunch. Bully Bear thundered through the factory floor, pushing all the other Stalkers out of the way as he wanted his food first.

"Grrrr . . .," growled Bully Bear, "I'm hungry! Give me more food!"

Being a greedy bully, he also stole portions of food from the young, inexperienced buzzards that were standing in line waiting for their breadcrumbs and water.

With the enemy Stalkers out of the way for a moment, and Vermont snoozing in the rafters, Devine flew with the Preps into Vermont's office. It was situated in the factory roof because Vermont liked to keep a close eye on everything. He was the head of all the evil operations and didn't trust anyone. The office was decorated in the worst possible taste. Comfort lined his plush golden nest, and there were plenty of bling accessories to feed his indulgent greed. The colours of the walls were loud, with curtains fit for a king's palace. He had a huge flat screen TV on the wall with every war game imaginable to play on his golden PlayStation.

Devine swiftly landed on a top secret file that had accidentally been left on Vermont's golden desk. The file contained a blueprint for the latest designs to change the seven robots that had been snatched by the buzzards from Dry Valley. The Preps quietly opened up the file and stared at the faulty robot plans. Oscar commented on how the designs for the wonky robots body did not match the description of the Church body which he had previously read about in his Bible.

Devine quickly flicked through the pages of his Bible to show the young Preps what God had to say about Vermont and the blueprint designs in his top secret file:

Matthew chapter 24 verses 4 to 14

The Master's words in the Bible confirmed what was behind Vermont's crafty plans.

Oscar liked being a spy, so he took a few photos of the robot blueprint plans using the camera on his mobile phone. No sooner had he clicked the button with his beak than it set off a loud ringtone on his phone. The noise was heard by all the Stalkers and buzzards as they ate their mean lunch in the canteen.

Stavros the saliva-dribbling fox never missed a trick. He was a sly and cunning Stalker. He leaped to his feet and charged through the factory canteen, knocking over all the workers' drinks with his long, bushy tail. With a loud thud, he sounded the intruder alarm. As the alarm bell rang in a piercing tone throughout the factory, the Stalkers ran around in disarray like buzzing bees. The buzzards just flapped their black wings in a rage. Another Stalker, Wiz the magical wizard lizard, decided to transport himself by magic into Vermont's office to help Stavros capture the unwanted guests. As Stavros came crashing through the office door he slipped on his sticky dribble and fell on top of Wiz.

The Preps would have liked to have seen a repeat performance of Stavros's grand entrance as it was hilarious. Instead, being wise, they used the opportunity to escape the attack. They sped away under the cover of light coming from Devine's tail feathers. The powerful light temporarily blinded the Stalkers, and the Preps escaped unharmed. As they flew across the back yard, the fat black rats were blown into a huddle beside the overflowing wheelie bins. The bins then began to roll and knocked over all the pursuing Stalkers.

Bully Bear broke one of his teeth in the chase. Reluctantly, he had to go and see the Stalker LuSINda the toothless lion for some urgent dental treatment. The other Stalkers noticed that he was not so big and brave when it came to going to the dentist. LuSINda used this opportunity to get back at the big bully by filling one of his broken teeth without any pain relief!

"Aghhh!" squealed Bully Bear, sobbing uncontrollably.

Vermont flew across the back yard in a rage, trying to control all the confusion going on in his Gift Factory. It took a whole day for the mayhem to calm down and for Bully Bear to stop crying.

Meanwhile, safely back in the Olive Grove, the Preps paused for breath and something to quench their thirst. There were some still waters flowing through the central garden in the Olive Grove, so they stopped there for a long, cool drink. With plenty of figs around too, they chewed on the luscious, sticky fruit to their hearts' content. Penny reminded the boys to wash their sticky beaks in the still waters after they had eaten. Full and satisfied, they prayed and gave thanks to Father God for their safe journey. Devine then left Oscar and Penny to look over the photos on Oscar's mobile phone. Afterwards, as extra homework, they keenly re-read the verses found in Matthew chapter 24.

"Don't be fooled!" remarked Penny as she finished the fascinating read. "We really need to be wise in everything we do because these are definitely difficult times."

The young Preps played late into the evening and then settled down to a well-earned rest, ready for the next day's adventures on this tricky, sticky trail.

5
Pretty Peacock

Before it was light, Penny woke up very excited. Oscar preferred to sleep and just like all growing teenagers he loved to lie in his nest for a few extra snoozes. Alone with her thoughts, Penny began star-gazing. As she stared up at the sky, something quite magical grabbed her attention. Seven big, bright, dazzling stars exploded in the dark, early morning sky. She had never seen anything quite like this before. These were very unusual times and even the heavens seemed to be getting ready for some kind of show. Penny stared carefully and while she did the stars got even brighter. There was no more containing her excitement – she gave Oscar the biggest peck possible with her tiny beak to wake him up.

"Ouch!" exclaimed Oscar. "What did you do that for?" he asked, fumbling around for his glasses.

Penny blushed and said, "Look at those seven stars. They seem to be sending out a message."

Perching his glasses on the end of his beak, Oscar looked more closely at the stars to see what his friend was so thrilled about. Suddenly, the seven stars fell and crashed into the landscape, giving an explosion of light. Star struck, the Preps couldn't sleep so they watched and waited for Devine to arrive so they could tell him all about the extraordinary happening.

Daylight seemed to take forever but as they watched for Devine it wasn't long before they saw his mighty wings fly like a canopy over the Olive Grove. Oscar and Penny kept interrupting each other as they rushed to tell Devine about their star-gazing. Devine smiled and explained how he had been on night watch in Blazing Glory and had taken part in the starry explosion.

"Last night, the Master called a very important meeting. You were able to see a picture of what he said because as you watched and prayed, heaven was opened like the curtains in a theatre and the seven stars were put on show as a sign of what is about to take place," said Devine excitedly. He then gave the meaning of what they had seen. "Only Father God knows the time when the Master will come back to earth. It's top secret. Even the Master, his Son Jesus, does not know when that will be. He waits excitedly for the day when his Father tells him to return. Jesus told me how little time there is left for the work of preparing his Church to be ready for Blazing Glory. He is coming for his Church very soon. The seven stars you saw represent the seven churches we are about to visit. They each contain one of the seven robots we saw being attacked as they tried to leave Dry Valley," Devine explained, like an expert teacher.

He turned the pages of his Bible to the last book, called Revelation, to find some very important words for the Preps to read. "This final book, full of hidden mysteries, tells the truth about how things will be at the end of time," Devine said. "It explains Father God's wonderful forever plan for those who have followed Jesus, the Master. However, those who have been tricked by Vermont will share in his terrible, fateful ending."

Oscar and Penny gasped as they picked up their magnifying glasses to read a description of Jesus.

Revelation chapter 1 verses 12 to 20

They read the verses with wonder and saw Jesus, the Master, in a new light. Oscar and Penny felt extremely honoured to be part of the special quest they were on. They were very glad that they were following the Master, and not Vermont. They were both determined to remain as Preps and not be tricked into becoming Pretenders. Ever keen to learn from Devine, the young Preps continued with their questions.

"I wonder whether the seven robots escaped unharmed from Dry Valley?" asked Penny.

"The buzzards' claws looked very sharp as they snatched the robots, but we did see two robots escape from their clutches," said Oscar with concern. He turned and looked up to Devine for his great insight.

"Two of the robots are doing well – no Pretenders attend the two churches where they are stationed. We just need to build the members of these two churches up with encouragement," said Devine, sounding hopeful. "But the other five robots do need urgent help in order to try and correct the wrong behaviour of the church members. I do hope we are not too late to use our influence to try to restore the five injured robots to full health before the Master returns," he exclaimed, with urgency in his voice.

Devine prayed with his students and asked for Father God's speed for their journey because the days were getting shorter and there was still so much work to be done.

With a short snack of skinny worms for breakfast, they broke the golden rule and flew on a full tummy of food. This made the flight uncomfortable for little Penny. She asked Oscar if they could land but the creeping mist was all over the ground so she had to push through the pain barrier and keep on going.

"Burp!" repeated the worms in Penny's tummy.

Penny blushed but her red cheeks did not compare to the vast array of bright colours which could now be seen in the distance. The multicoloured feathers they could see belonged to the peacocks that were in charge of the first church in Ephesus. The sight cheered up Penny as she loved bright colours. Oscar was happy as they were nearly at their destination, especially because Penny's wind problem was making the flight more and more uncomfortable. Ephesus was a bit of a big name for little birds to say, so they decided to call it the 'Epee Centre' instead.

As they landed at the Epee Centre church they received a spectacular welcome. Inside the multicoloured church there were flashing lights hip-hopping around the walls. The light show bounced around the platform, and the whole church blazed in light and colour. Loud music was being pumped out of the huge music speakers. This had attracted a large gathering of birds and the crowds were going crazy.

Unusually, Devine chose to land at the back of the crowd, soon followed by Oscar and Penny. A huge flock of birds immediately swarmed around Devine as they queued up to get a powerful touch from his wings. Sadly no-one even noticed Oscar, let alone little Penny.

Waiting in the sidelines, the two young Preps watched the behaviour of the birds in the church. They remembered that they were to be on watch for any Pretenders in the ranks. It was hard to tell as everyone appeared to be doing the right thing while they were in the building. As they waited for Devine, they looked at all the jazzy posters which lined the colourful walls.

"Feast your bird's-eye on this!" cried stunned Oscar.

"Crumbs!" replied Penny. "Those colourful feathers are the most stunning I have ever seen in my short little life!"

Both Oscar and Penny was mesmerised by the Epee Centre's star-quality leader, Priscilla the peacock. Her pretty poster was everywhere.

"I'm impressed. Priscilla has been awarded a five-star rating for her weekly speeches," remarked Oscar.

"Do you think the Master will be impressed if her pretty words just tickle the listeners' ears with fancy feathers?" responded Penny.

Suddenly, the audience of birds scrambled and pushed to

find a perch to sit down on. The Preps thought they must all be getting ready for Devine to address them with the special message in the letter he was carrying from Blazing Glory. To their surprise, Devine hovered at the back of the church. Sadly, he had been left out of the order of service and wouldn't be given a chance to speak.

With a magnificent warm-up announcement, the crowd stood to their feet and applauded Priscilla, the most spectacular peacock. She dazzled them all with her feathers as she came on stage. Waiting for the applause to stop, she made herself ready to talk by brushing her colourful feathers. The crowd then made themselves comfortable on rows of bird perches, ready to listen to her five-star speech. Oddly, instead of speaking about matters found in her Bible she seemed to prefer to talk about her beautiful feathers

and how her feathers were attracting a great crowd of admirers.

"My, how she loves to show off her colourful feathers," remarked Penny, transfixed by the glamorous scene.

Oscar was a little wiser than Penny and he was certainly not into dressing up. Using his gift of wisdom, he checked for fruit being displayed by Priscilla's actions. Sadly, he could not find the fruit badges on her splendid feathers, nor was there any sign of the eight Be-attitude stripes.

Devine sighed and then made a swift exit out of the room. He was going to find out where the wonky robot was hiding, and after that he would wait for the right moment to speak to the gathering, soon after Priscilla had finished her talk. The Preps quickly followed as they couldn't bear to watch the performance on the stage any longer.

As they all flapped around the corridors, bumping into one another because they were in such a hurry to find the robot, Devine suddenly beckoned with his wing. "Over here," he whispered. "The Pretenders have hidden the robot in Priscilla's dressing room. We'll have to sneak in quietly and work very fast to identify the robot's problems before Priscilla returns from the stage."

On first sight, the large robot looked amazing. It was brightly coloured, with flashing lights and sparkling panels, and was covered in expensive jewellery. However, upon closer examination with their magnifying glasses, they discovered that its arms were missing and had been replaced by lots of ears.

"This injury must have happened when it was captured by Vermont and the buzzards as it came out of Dry Valley," said Penny with great surprise.

However, the damage had remained unnoticed by those

who attended the Epee Centre church, due to the spangly earrings decorating the ears.

"Maybe it had some plastic surgery at the Gift Factory and that's how the arms have been replaced by so many pairs of ears," suggested Penny. "Vermont has tried to cover things up with the lovely earrings so that people won't realise what he's up to."

The shiny jewellery made the robot more attractive, giving it worldly appeal. Unfortunately, those responsible for maintaining the robot had failed to see the faults because they were so dazzled by the jewellery. The fact they had fallen for Vermont's trick of covering over the robot's faults showed that the Epee Centre church members had become Pretenders and were covering up their own faults, trying to look good on the outside. The well-trained Preps, however, had spotted the problem straight away.

Following Devine's lead, they carefully tested all the robot's other body parts, which seemed to be in the right place. Then, Devine's searching eyes found a minor defect. All the little toes were missing.

"The toes bring balance to the robot's body and they are very important," exclaimed Devine. "But the fact that they are missing tells us something about the attitude of the church members. The toes represent those who quietly get on and do the small, everyday jobs in the church, like the cleaning, making the tea, and so on. But the more important body parts, in other words, the people holding jobs that seem more important, have dismissed these folk as useless.

"That's not very nice," said an upset Penny. "Everyone in a church is useful, and all the jobs that get done are equally as important as each other."

You're absolutely right," responded Devine, pleased that his young student had learnt so much already. "Since everything appears good on the outside of the robot, it looks as if the church members are doing everything right. That's why the robot is so colourful, glitzy and covered in shiny ornaments. But, just because it's big and colourful doesn't mean that everything is going well inside the hearts of the folk here. It's clear that those who attend this church are becoming Pretenders in their worship of Father God," said Devine with great sorrow.

Priscilla the peacock had plenty to say that day and there seemed to be no time left for Devine to bring the important message from Blazing Glory to the audience. The Preps watched and waited with Devine only to find that Priscilla, along with a trail of copy-cat peacocks, had left the church to go for their expensive Sunday lunch. Only followers who admired her speeches and feathers were allowed to be part of the feast. With the church almost empty, Oscar and Penny flew back inside. They found just a handful of the flock of birds sweeping up the mess left by the entertained crowd. These birds had remained as Preps and had not become Pretenders. They noticed Devine coming in and watched as he landed on the lampstand at the front of the church. This lampstand was the most prized possession of the church. It gave light and hope to the birds that were waiting for the Master's return.

"It's no use, I will have to remove this lampstand if the church members do not change their ways," said Devine reluctantly but firmly.

Gray the head server, a plump little pigeon, was shocked as he overheard Devine's warning. He shed a few grey feathers in dismay and bowed his head as he began to speak to Devine.

"Please do not take the lampstand. This is our only hope for change. When the lamp is alight we know that Jesus is with us and is watching over us," said Gray. "Can you please help us to change our pretending ways so that the lampstand can remain?" he pleaded, as all the other serving pigeons nodded in agreement.

There were lots of things that the Epee Centre church members were doing right but, sadly, they had forgotten so many of Father God's ways. They were listening to long speeches about their leader, but not about God. They had become picky about the words in their Bibles, and selected only the bits they liked to obey, while they ignored very simple instructions about how to be kind and put each other first.

Priscilla liked the look of the new robot that Vermont had created, and she was allowing the damaged robot to affect the behaviour of the members, which she made worse by leading them in pretending ways. When the robot had lost its toes, Priscilla had just shrugged her shoulders because she thought the little members in the church were unimportant. The missing arms showed that instead of raising their wings in worship to God, the members were now giving that worship to Priscilla the Pretender, who was more in love with herself than God and those around her. The shiny earrings on the ears that had replaced the robot's arms showed that the followers were being tricked into only looking at the glitzy outside, rather than what was on the inside. Regrettably, most of the members of the Epee Centre church had lost their first love, which was to love and worship Father God.

Being kind and merciful, Devine decided to give the members of the Epee Centre church one more chance to get things right. He called for an urgent meeting with Priscilla in the Olive Grove near the church. Sadly, she refused to attend because she said the oil would mess up her pretty feathers. Instead she sent her personal assistant, Prudence, with a feeble excuse. Devine explained to Prudence the urgency of the hour and commanded that Priscilla and the church members must return to loving Father God and loving others before themselves. Sternly, Devine ordered that the two arms must be put back onto the robot and that the church leaders must give more importance to the little members of the flock.

The personal assistant's pretty feathers turned a pale shade of grey as she wondered how this message could be carried to Priscilla without upsetting her. Prudence looked sad as she left. How she dreaded speaking anything other than flattery to Priscilla. Priscilla couldn't stand being told anything unless it was about how good her feathers looked! Behind her back she was more commonly known as Prickly Priscilla.

For the sake of the Preps attending the Epee Centre church, Devine called a meeting in the Olive Grove for those who were ready to change. As they waited for the birds to arrive, Devine opened his Bible so that Oscar and Penny could read the special letter from Blazing Glory that described the Epee Centre church's problems:

Revelation chapter 2 verses 1 to 7

An air of sadness breezed through the Olive Grove as Oscar and Penny read about the great possibilities for the church, which would only happen if they changed their feathery ways. Devine knew that Priscilla would find it extremely hard to make herself less self-centred because she had become used to all the attention being focused on her. But that was no excuse for a bad attitude, which would never be allowed in Blazing Glory.

One by one, hundreds of seemingly unimportant birds flocked to the Olive Grove. They all perched high up in the trees because Vermont was sending in his creeping mist to try and put the watching birds to sleep. His Stalkers were not allowed inside the Olive Grove but there were always plenty of Pretenders who would keep them well informed of any zealous Preps. As you can imagine, Pretenders are prize gossips. Devine welcomed the birdwatchers and then read the letter to them.

As Devine shuddered with the seriousness of the moment, a feather fluttered to the ground, carrying instructions that would help them to change.

2 Timothy chapter 2 verse 15

"It is very important to learn to use the living words in your Bible in the right way and to apply the words correctly. Think about it like this. Your arms are there to be raised upwards in worship to Father God and also to reach outwards to give help and blessing to all," said Devine. "Freely you have received . . . and so freely give. When your arms take everything for yourself, your worship becomes of no use. God has given the Epee Centre church great benefits for you to share with others, and the Bible says that to those who have been given much, much will be required. Follow the right way, the better way of love, because when your gifts are no more it will be love which remains. Character, not gifts, is rewarded in Blazing Glory."

The birdwatchers were moved by Devine's words and promised to work to put things right. Devine sent a written copy of the message to Priscilla and stressed her need to change. One day she would be judged for the way she had led those in her care, so it was very important for her to lead in a right way. She had to change if she was ever to enter Blazing Glory.

When word got back to Priscilla about the meeting, she was in a colourful rage.

"How can he threaten to take away my most beautiful lampstand?" Priscilla bellowed as her language became even more colourful. "I'll, I'll. . .!" shouted the peacock as large bright feathers were shed in anger from her tail.

But in her heart of hearts, Priscilla knew that if the lampstand was removed then the Epee Centre church would eventually close, especially once her colourful, ageing feathers had lost their appeal. Sitting and staring at her beautiful feathers in the mirror, she reflected on how she loved herself more than others. Whether she would do anything about the warning, one day time would tell. While she considered her ways and the way in which the Epee Centre church chose to operate, the other watching birds gained strength in the oil found in their own personal time in the Olive Grove. They clutched onto this feather of hope sent by Father God, who was watching over them:

Psalm 16 verse 3

6
Warring Birds

"What a colourful day," declared Penny as they took off, having completed the first flight mission of this epic tale.

"I do hope things will get better at the next church," said Oscar with a heavy sigh as they soared full steam ahead.

With a long journey before them, Devine took the young Preps for a light afternoon refreshment at an Olive Grove service station on the highway. They landed at the 'fly through zone' to instantly enjoy some pre-picked figs and a cool drink of ice-cold water. Being young birds, they loved fast food. Devine talked to the birds about the next church they were going to visit as they munched on their lunch and slurped on their chilled drinks.

"This church houses one of the two robots that escaped the mean clutches of Vermont and the buzzards in Dry Valley. It was a very courageous robot and wrestled long and hard in a brave fight. Daringly, it got away and escaped the Gift Factory. Unfortunately, since the robot's victory, the church where it's stationed has remained under continued attack from Vermont and his nasty bandits," said Devine proudly.

"I thought if you did good works then everything would

automatically go well," commented Oscar with a puzzled frown.

Penny just scratched her head with her claw as this also made her a little confused.

Devine explained how this was quite the opposite. "Think about the things that the Master, Jesus, experienced when he walked the earth as a man, and how many people were against the good things that he did. The pages of your Bible are full of stories showing how Jesus was persecuted, especially by religious people," replied Devine.

"Devine, what does pers-, perse-, 'persecuted' mean?" asked Penny, having trouble pronouncing this long word.

"It means that people were nasty to Jesus. They didn't like what he was doing, even though he was only doing good things, so they gave him a hard time."

Seeing that the young Preps were still concerned and puzzled, Devine poured some oil from the olive trees into the tiny tube pots on their wings, to help them understand things more easily.

Then he asked Penny to open and read the following Bible verses:

1 Peter chapter 4 verses 12 to 19

The pages of the open Bible fluttered in the breeze as she read. Oscar noticed how Penny was quickly becoming a great teacher who not only communicated well but also led by good example. She was turning out to be quite an impressive student in Devine's book, too. From the Bible verses they now understood that persecution would also await them on the journey. Oscar and Penny were happy to be ill-treated in the same way as Jesus because it meant they would grow to be more like him, but they were a little scared and realised that they needed his help to be brave, so they prayed together.

Then they took off, hoping to make the evening service at the church which was being persecuted. As expected, the flight was extremely dangerous. The mist was thicker than they had ever seen before and this made seeing very difficult. Devine reminded the Preps about the oil in their pouches, which could be used on such hazardous occasions. Oscar and Penny were glad they had topped up their oil at the last Olive Grove as they needed the extra supply. Amazingly, as they prayed, the oil was set alight and shone like lamps. A warm feeling filled their hearts at that moment because they knew Father God was pleased with their progress and was with them in a special way, even though they couldn't see him.

They were not far from the persecuted church when the air space became very unsafe and bumpy.

"Watch out!" cried Penny as they dodged threatening missiles.

Stones were being thrown by the enemies hidden in the mist, who had detected the flying Preps. The stones were being thrown not by the Stalkers but by religious Pretenders who had been badly affected by the mist. Confusion encircled Oscar like a cloud, and he began to have trouble believing he could fly the distance to reach their destination.

"I thought we were on the same side!" cried Oscar, extremely upset and confused, his tears washing over his friend and passenger, Penny.

Devine could see the danger they were in and so called

them up to higher air thermals and insisted they carried on. He instructed them to watch and pray as they kept flying forwards, dodging any random stones that was thrown. The stones were actually just words of doubt and fear which would eventually tumble to the ground.

"Don't take the bad words on board!" Oscar shouted to Penny. "They will only bring us down."

Pushing through the word attack, they headed towards the city of Smyrna below. Oscar decided to circle the city a few times as he couldn't believe how grand the church was in the city centre below. It was decorated with marble pillars and its round dome was layered with gold. The Preps thought they had arrived at the persecuted church. Unsure of where Devine was in the thick mist, the Preps looked in their Bibles to see what it said about this place and what was contained in its special message from Blazing Glory. Happily, they had their bright lamps glowing on their wings, acting like super torches to help them see the words.

Revelation chapter 2 verses 8 to 11

Remarkably, Devine had flown past the golden church in a hurry. He realised the young Preps had been delayed, so he sent a message to them on the secret winds. "Keep flying onwards and upwards," he called. "The golden building is one of Vermont's plush palaces. It is not the persecuted church. You are in great danger."

Hearing the news, Oscar flew as quickly as he could with Penny holding tightly onto his feathery back so that he could catch up with Devine. They continued for a few more miles and were surprised to see Devine landing at a shabby church building. This was in fact where the persecuted friends of the Master met in secret.

"This can't be right," marvelled Penny, as they touched down right next to Devine.

"They may look poor but really they are rich!" smiled Devine with great pride.

Cheerfully, a massive crowd had begun to assemble in secret. As they were persecuted, they had to meet in secret so as not to attract the attention of those who wanted to destroy them. They had to keep meeting in different buildings around the city of Smyrna, so that they wouldn't be discovered by Vermont or any Pretenders. Directions to the church's latest location were always sent on the secret winds so that all Preps in the city could hear where they were to meet.

"It's a bit like Hide and Seek," laughed Oscar and Penny, enjoying making the dangerous adventure into a fun game.

It wasn't a fun game for those who risked their lives to meet together as the persecuted church. All the Preps in this city had understood that if Jesus had suffered persecution through doing everything right, then they must expect – and even be glad about – suffering in the same way as their Master.

Guarding the church door was a strange-looking eagle. He looked like he could have been Oscar's long-lost uncle. This was Pablo, the bald eagle, who was expecting Devine's visit and was waiting with great anticipation. He welcomed his visitors with a big wing-hug and Devine introduced them to one another.

"Pablo is a very dear and wise friend," explained Devine to the young Preps. "He has quite a pedigree. As a young eagle,

he attended the High Flyers Academy, where he was one of their top students. He saw first-hand the beginnings of the early Church. After Jesus the Master had returned to Blazing Glory, his followers continued with the work of spreading the Good News about him to the whole world. Pablo flew after them and watched and followed their adventures, along with his fellow-student Pedro the kingfisher. Pablo was particularly interested in the life of the great apostle and missionary, Paul. Pedro the kingfisher, whom I will hopefully introduce you to soon, spent most of his time studying the life of another great apostle, Peter."

With the introductions over and done with, Pablo stepped forward and informed the Preps of the great danger in the city of Smyrna.

"'I-Spy' is the code name of this church," Pablo whispered

in a very deep tone. He coughed, putting his large wing politely over his crooked beak. He did this so that he could not be overheard by any watching Stalker or Pretender who might be lurking down the dark, misty streets. Oscar and Penny loved this name as they enjoyed playing the game I-Spy on long journeys. But this quest was no game.

Pablo had some alarming news for Devine. He explained how Pedro the kingfisher had flown away on a special mission to spread the Good News about Jesus but unfortunately he had been arrested and put in prison by the buzzards. The incredible thing was that the apostle Peter, Pedro's Bible hero, had also been arrested and put in prison many years before. The birds had all come to the I-Spy church to pray for Pedro's safety. Pablo wasn't sure if, or when, Pedro would come back but he had decided to remain at the persecuted church for a time to encourage those who were being bullied for their faith in Jesus.

Oscar was a bit baffled by the tricky situation and asked Pablo if there were any Pretenders hiding or working in this church.

"Strangely enough, persecution and hard times seem to bring everyone together. You cannot fake being a Christian when you understand that the call to follow the Master demands everything, even your popularity and reputation," commented Pablo. "So I don't think any Pretenders will be hiding in this place because the persecuted birds take the call very seriously."

"The call? I thought the call was to watch?" said Penny, a little perplexed.

"To watch means we must believe that the events Jesus said would happen at the Last Hour, will happen, and we need to be ready for them. He promised to look after us, but he also clearly warned us how only tested faith will be rewarded in Blazing Glory," replied Pablo, who had been tested many times and on many occasions for his faith in Jesus Christ.

Devine explained that real Preps must always check out information in their manuals for themselves. So he told them to look up the following verses, where they could read that what Pablo had just said was true:

Matthew chapter 24 verses 9 to 14

The persecuted church found great comfort in these words, which helped them through the difficult times they had to face. When Penny read the words more closely again, she was amazed. She wanted to be like the Preps here at the I-Spy church because they had been promised a crown in Blazing Glory!

"I would do *anything* to win a crown," sighed dreamy Penny.

As Pedro the kingfisher was in prison, Devine decided to pay him a visit with Oscar and Penny.

"Visiting those who are in need is all part of what Jesus wants his waiting Church to be doing when he returns," smiled Devine.

Swiftly, they left the shabby church by the back door so they wouldn't be seen by any Pretenders or any of Vermont's dastardly crew.

Always on the lookout for a victim, the ever-nasty Bully Bear was lurking down a side street. The bully had become bored waiting and had started to play noisy games, annoying the local residents. He was angrily kicking a can around, waiting for his prey. The can made a loud racket as it rolled down the pebbly streets. Fortunately for the Preps, the bully missed their exit because he was distracted by the clattering sound of his dented can. Being wise birds, they flew above the mist which was creeping down the dark winding alley towards the prison house. As they got closer, they could hear singing.

Oscar thought it was very strange for prisoners to be singing in prison. "How can anyone be happy in such dark and damp conditions?" remarked Oscar as he perched outside the prison.

Green moss covered the outside of the prison, like a slimy coat. Fortunately, because their feathers were oily, Oscar and Penny were able to slide through the slim prison bar windows. They squeezed through and searched to find where Pedro had been chained up. Peering into a dark, dingy cell, Penny gave a huge gasp because she couldn't believe her tiny eyes. Who should also be locked up in prison but Jack the jackdaw, one of the long-lost Dupes from the *Trick or Treat?* adventure!

Immediately, Oscar and Penny flew over to him and gave him an extra-long wing-hug. Jack was so glad to see some friendly faces. He had made friends with Pedro the kingfisher, his cell-mate. Pedro was very good at fishing for friends with the Good News about Jesus. Jack remembered his time at the Camp of Life with Oscar and Penny. Sadly, he had followed Vermont down the wrong path which had led to a dead end. He had given up hope of things ever changing because he had spent so much time in and out of prison. However, he had learnt from his mistakes and he was now ready to hear about the right way to Blazing Glory.

"Cor, your wings are beautiful, Penny!" commented Jack. "Where did you get all those fruit badges from? And what are those stripes that are shining across your feathers?"

"Thank you, Jack. You will be able to earn your own badges as you follow the right way to Blazing Glory," smiled Penny, extremely pleased that she now had some of the Be-attitude stripes.

While Jack spent time admiring the fruit badges on the young Prep's wings, Devine spent time with Pedro and began to clean the wounds on his back. Pedro had been badly beaten by the buzzard prison guards, and some of the feathers on his back had been torn off. As Devine applied oil to Pedro's back, the wounds began to heal and the colour of the Be-attitude stripes came through instead. Jack, Oscar and Penny were amazed by the transformation.

A feather floated down from the sky. The words on it showed the young Preps why Pedro's heroic behaviour would be rewarded in Blazing Glory.

Matthew chapter 5 verse 10

Remarkably, Pedro was happy and blessed, even in his chains. He did not mind being chained up for spreading the gospel but instead found it to be a great privilege to do this for his Master, Jesus.

Pedro, being a kingfisher, wanted everyone to share in his joy and so he began to sing at the top of his voice all about Jesus. Unexpectedly, the ground began to shake as Devine roared with laughter. As the ground shook, the chains on all the prisoners began to rattle and then to everyone's amazement they fell off and crashed to the ground. The mean-looking buzzard prison guards came rushing over and then froze on the spot as the prison doors were flung open. The doors knocked the guards clean out and put them to sleep with a thud!

All the prisoners were now free. The Preps were overjoyed to have witnessed the great escape. Pedro the kingfisher left the prison house along with Oscar, Penny and Devine, while the newly converted Jack followed swiftly behind them. He had decided to say sorry and repent of his old ways, wanting now to follow Jesus along the way to Blazing Glory. Under the cover of light, they all flew back to the shabby church building which housed and trained the persecuted church members.

"Knock, knock," was heard on the tatty church door.

A tubby little robin called Rhoda came to answer the door.

"Who's there?" asked Rhoda, as she stood on the tips of her claws to try and peer through the peep-hole in the door.

When she saw Pedro, she turned round and wobbled with joy back into the room where the others were meeting.

"It's Pedro, it's Pedro at the door!" squealed Rhoda. "Yippee! Hallelujah!" she cried, forgetting to open the door as she was so excited that he had escaped from prison.

Pedro's freedom was an answer to all their prayers. Pablo went and opened the church door after peering through the I-Spy peep-hole, just in case this was a trap set by Vermont. When he saw it really was Pedro, he flung the door wide open and everyone celebrated the happy sight. They were also all thrilled to welcome Jack as a new member of the I-Spy church. Welcoming new friends to the I-Spy church had become a daily event.

Later, Pablo announced that he had decided to fly away as Pedro had come back and could look after the church in his place. Pablo asked Devine if he could join him and the young Preps on their journey because he wanted to meet up with Tiny Tim the blue tit. Tiny Tim would be at one of the other churches that Devine was set to visit. Devine and the Preps were more than happy for Pablo to join them on their special mission, especially as his age and experience would be of great help to the young, learning birds.

Before they left, the young Preps took the opportunity to find and examine the robot in the I-Spy church. Oscar especially wanted to do this as boys really love transforming robots. They found the robot in the boiler room, exactly where it should be.

They eagerly got out their magnifying glasses and peered at the outside of the robot, using the lights in their wing pouches to help them see. Both Preps were inspired by the fine example of what a good robot should look like. The power driving the robot was the power of Jesus. Although the I-Spy robot was a bit shabby, it possessed every body part described in their manuals. And each body part was in the correct place and was working as it should. This was a sign of what the real Church should look like. It meant that every church member was happy in their set place. This was what made them rich. They were rich in love because their hands embraced everyone who came in. None of them was trying to be more important than the others, because they all knew that they needed one another. This was important to remember if they were going to survive the persecution surrounding the true Church in the Last Hour.

Devine gladly blessed the gathering of birds as he gently handed Pedro the letter from Blazing Glory. He took off into the starry night sky followed by Oscar, Penny and Pablo the bald eagle. They flew outside the city and landed in the nearest  Olive Grove to find oil for their tube pots and to nest and rest. As they nestled down for the night, Pablo, who loved to talk, told the two young Preps many of the exciting missionary tales of his Bible hero, the apostle Paul. The tales were full of daring adventures and miraculous escapes. Paul had spent his life taking the Good News about Jesus into the whole world, and was even prepared to die doing it.

Penny tried to stay awake for as long as Oscar but soon she was sound asleep. Whoever said that girls talk more than boys?

7
Half-Way House

It was a very noisy night in the Olive Grove. Pablo, the bald eagle, had a small problem with the nostrils in his beak which meant that he snored! His snore was a big snore because he had such a large crooked beak. The only birds that could sleep near to Pablo were a small family of ostriches who buried their heads in the soil to escape the noisy racket. Burying their heads to find peace and quiet wasn't an option for Oscar and Penny. Instead, they politely moved to a very green and leafy branch lower down the tree. The leaves acted like a soundproof blanket so they were able to get back to sleep.

Pablo was undisturbed by the din of his own snoring and had a good night's rest. He was up at the crack of dawn as he had a nest-making business and had work to do. The nests he made with his own claws were no ordinary nests. His nests were ones which could be transported like tents for birds who loved to migrate. He did this in his spare time so that he could afford to travel to lots of different places with the Good News about Jesus. Pablo got on with his work quietly.

All of a sudden there was a loud 'pop' as the ostriches pulled their heads out of the soil because the snoring had finally stopped. The popping noise woke up Oscar and Penny, who busily began to fill up their oil tube pots ready for the day's adventure. As they finished, they began to pray, and with a quick prayer response Devine swooped into the Olive Grove.

"Good morning, my friends," said Devine.

"Aghhh . . . good morning," responded Penny as she stretched her wings and yawned at the same time.

Devine called the three Preps together and discussed with them their next 'fowl' journey. Yes, it was a 'fowl' place because they were going to fly to Turkey. Pablo knew this was a tough assignment as he had travelled there before, during his days at the High Flyers Academy. Due to the heat, he suggested to the group that they stop off at a half-way house he knew called 'Manna Farm'.

"Sounds like it's a house full of fresh bread," commented clever Oscar.

"Yummy!" responded hungry Penny, who liked to break up the journey with a spot to eat.

Pablo then began to tell the others how this half-way house had been started many years before. He was proud to have been there himself, perched up on the roof, when it had opened. It was built so that the Christian community could distribute help and food to the poor. Its founder member was a man called Stephen. Stephen was the first Christian to be martyred for his faith in Jesus, the Master.

"What does the big word 'martyr' mean?" quivered Penny as her feathers began to shake.

As Pablo answered her question, a tear ran down his beak and splashed on the ground. Sensitively, Devine continued with the tale so that Pablo could compose himself. Pablo took a big deep breath to which Penny responded with a gentle stroke of Pablo's bald head. Devine opened his Bible and asked Penny to use her magnifying glass to help her read the story about the hero Stephen. She would learn from his example that a martyr is someone who dies for their faith in Jesus.

Acts chapter 7 verses 51 to 60

It was a moving story which showed the Preps how they must also be prepared to lay down their lives in a selfless way for the Master. At that precise moment, a feather with the following Bible verse on it fluttered from Devine's wing:

John chapter 15 verse 13

Pablo, with great sorrow, told the others how he had been there, watching from a tree, when Stephen had been stoned. In fact, he was especially sorry because his hero Paul had been one of those who had taken part in the terrible attack. At that time, both Paul and Pablo had been on the side of the Pretenders.

"Gasp!" went Penny. She had not been this close to someone who had been a Pretender before.

"Gulp!" sounded Oscar, swallowing hard at the news.

With such a colourful story, even the ostriches in the Olive Grove stretched their necks high into the air so that they could listen too. These unusual-looking birds liked to stretch their necks in suspense and were almost as nosey as parrots.

"Don't worry," said Pablo quickly, seeing their alarmed faces. "After seeing Stephen's act of great courage, Paul the missionary began to consider his ways and so did I. One day, during my training with the High Flyers Academy, I followed Paul on a long and dusty journey to a place called Damascus. There he was blinded by the Master with a blazing ray of light. From this extraordinary meeting with Jesus, he realised how he had been blind to the truth about Father God and how to get to Blazing Glory. After a few long days, God gave him his sight back again so that he could tell people about Jesus, and that's what he spent the rest of his life doing. It was at this point that I too decided to change my ways and tell others about Jesus. I realised that I could live and maybe even die, like the great martyr Stephen, for this noble cause," spoke Pablo with great strength of conviction.

"He's not just bald on his head but bold in his belief," whispered Oscar to Penny as they marvelled at the tale.

The two young Preps were not used to real-life stories and real-life heroes. They waited for a moment to consider what they may or may not encounter along the way ahead of them. Pablo then opened the way in prayer, ready for the birds to take flight.

With Devine at the front of the flight path and Pablo protecting the young Preps at the rear, they rose into the skies with great confidence. As they approached their next destination, Pergamum City, thick black clouds began to collect in front of them like a huge wall.

"'Mum's' the code word for this city," said Devine. "Remember, 'Mum's' the word!"

"Phew," went Penny, as this name was much shorter and easier to pronounce than Pergamum!

"This is a tough region. It's Vermont's home town," continued Devine.

"Yikes!" squawked Oscar.

"Double yikes!" copied Penny.

Oscar began to tremble at the thought and Penny held on for dear life to the feathers on Oscar's back. Oscar was starting to long for the day when his passenger, Penny, could fly as fast and as far as he could. "But maybe that day will never arrive," thought Oscar, "as my wings will always be bigger than those of a small sparrow."

Pablo noticed the danger they were in, so he descended underneath the young Preps and stretched out his extra-long eagle-wings to carry them on his back to the half-way house. Carrying each other's burdens was something Pablo had mastered through his many challenges along the way to Blazing Glory.

As they were all working together, Father God commanded the huge black wall of clouds to open up in front of them. The black clouds broke and poured out raindrops in a mighty rush, clearing the flight path to Manna Farm. Penny chuckled because she could now see how everything, even bad things, work together for good when you follow the Master. The rain shower had also cleared away the mist surrounding Manna Farm, creating a clear runway for Pablo to land on with his extra cargo, Oscar and Penny.

Manna Farm was a wood-panelled chicken barn. The birds living on this farm were part of the big church in Mum City. They were the freedom flyers based in the large group of growing Pretenders that went to the church. Never giving up their freedom, this small group of Preps produced free range eggs to help feed and serve the local community. The chicken barn was named after Stephen the martyr because he had started this good work many years before. In the fields to the back of the barn was a large white memorial stone which had written on it the names of all those who had been martyred for their faith in Jesus Christ. Stephen's name was top of the list because he was the first to follow Jesus and die in this way.

As they landed, they were greeted with loud clucking from a lot of noisy hens and chickens. Ever watchful, the two young Preps climbed down off Pablo's long, strong back and kept a sharp eye open for any Pretenders amongst the clucking birds. During all the noisy commotion, Pablo slipped away to be alone. Penny gazed round and saw him standing with his bald head hung down in front of the large white memorial stone. He was clutching onto a tatty piece of cloth.

"What's Pablo holding?" enquired Penny.

"It's a piece of the cloak that belonged to Stephen. It was left at Paul's feet after Stephen was stoned to death. Paul carried it with him on all his missionary trails, and one day a piece tore off on a prickly bush and Pablo swooped down and picked it up in his beak. He now carries it with him wherever he goes to remind him that Stephen gave his life for the Master, Jesus," explained Devine.

Suddenly, there was a very loud clatter. Who should come wafting into the farmyard but that trendy chick, Delilah, from the *Trick or Treat?* adventure. She looked quite out of place around the ordinary group of birds that lived on Manna Farm. The noise caught Pablo's attention, so he quickly dried his weepy eyes on the tatty scrap of cloth and rejoined the group.

"Why, why, why Delilah, we did not expect to see you here," smiled Oscar as he lifted Penny up so they could both give her a warm wing-hug.

The last time they had seen Delilah was at the Camp of Life. She had followed the Dupes down the wrong path. Ever since, Penny and Oscar had both been wondering how, or if, she had managed to find her way back onto the road of truth leading to Blazing Glory. They were pleased to see that it seemed as if she had.

Delilah didn't say how or when this had happened but just talked about her great new job. Delilah was a member of the changing Mum City church. She worked very closely with the leader, Nicolas the senior rooster. Nicolas was more fondly known as Nikey Nick. He had started off leading the church really well. However, as this was Vermont's home town there was no shortage of menacing mist and the poisonous fumes had rapidly begun to change Nikey Nick who had now developed a split personality. To make things worse, many of the church members had become sleepy from the effects of the mist. They weren't paying enough attention to the detail in the Bible and were now just blindly following Nikey Nick.

"What's a split personality?" asked curious Penny.

"One minute you are good and then you are bad," replied

Devine. "He's a rooster who sits on the fence when he makes his decisions. He loves to please the crowd."

"I do hope he doesn't wobble because he may well fall off and land on the wrong side," chuckled little Penny.

Devine turned to some verses in the Bible to show the Preps how someone like Nikey Nick changes their mind all the time, just to please others.

James chapter 1 verses 7 & 8

"A leader mustn't be like that because their actions must match their words. As they are in a high position, the majority in the group will follow their behaviour. Those who do not read their Bibles at home are especially likely to be fooled by crafty behaviour. It all becomes a bit like the game Follow the Leader," responded Devine, trying to help the young Preps understand the fault.

"Oh, I get it," said Penny, very pleased with herself.

Pablo didn't need to look up the verses as he knew the words off by heart. Being a modest bald eagle he didn't show off with his knowledge but allowed Penny to read the verse out loud and develop her growing gift of teaching, although secretly he would have preferred Oscar to read because he was a boy. Instead, he closed his beak, put his tongue in his cheek and was actually very impressed with little Penny!

"Let's go and take a look at the robot in the Mum City church and deliver my message to Nikey Nick," suggested Devine. "We can then see for ourselves if he has made his mind up whom he will serve – Vermont or the Master."

Devine gently asked Delilah to escort them to the church because she had a special pass to access any part of the building. They flew over the crawling mist before landing on top of the church spire and squeezing into the building through a small hole in the roof where one of the tiles had fallen off.

"If you don't mind," Devine said to Delilah, "we'll just have a little fly about inside. Thanks for helping us to get in."

Delilah winked and flashed one of her dazzling smiles before swooping off, leaving Devine and the Preps to get on with their important detective work. In the corner of the building was a rotating door which they decided to try. As they pushed the door, it swivelled round and round very fast, and the birds landed in a confused heap on the floor in the room on the other side.

Picking themselves up and dusting themselves down, to their amazement the birds found a tall, two-headed robot gazing down at them. They were now even more confused.

"No wonder the members of this church can't make their mind up deciding the right way to go," remarked Pablo as he flew up to sit on the smiling robot head which looked forwards.

The others glided up to the other robot head which was looking backwards and wearing a large frown.

"Ha, ha, ha . . . take a long look at the eyes on this robot's head! It keeps winking," chattered little Penny.

"You can't trust someone who winks," piped up clever Oscar, remembering that he had just seen Delilah give them a big wink, too.

The frowning head that winked had been fixed on by the Night Wolf at the Gift Factory after the robot had been captured leaving Dry Valley. Nikey Nick liked the two-headed robot and had turned a blind eye to the problem.

Upon closer inspection, the Preps also noticed that the robot had no fingers. During the buzzard attack in Dry Valley, the fingers had been pulled off. Without the fingers, the church members had begun to stop paying attention to the smaller important details of the church operations. They had become clumsy at handling situations and they no longer stood up for the things they knew to be true.

Just when the Preps thought it couldn't get any worse, Devine showed them a grim condition found on the robot's back. The robot had no backbone because it had been affected by the menacing mist hanging over Mum City. The spine had begun to crumble when Nikey Nick became too friendly with Vermont and his Stalkers. As Nikey Nick was now working for both the Master and Vermont, it was only a matter of time before the robot would totally crumble and fall crashing to the ground.

"You can only serve one master," said Pablo with great authority on the matter. "A house which is divided in its loyalty will fall. This one certainly looks like it's crumbling."

Very concerned, Devine decided it was time to go and see naughty Nick. The little group made their way back out through the rotating door into the main part of the church, this time being a lot more careful not to whizz round so quickly. They spotted Delilah perched in one of the pews, applying lipstick to her beak. Devine called over to her to ask her to lead them to Nikey Nick's office. She hurriedly bundled her lipstick under her wing, and agreed to take them.

As they followed, they noticed that the whole place was showing signs of falling apart. They flew up into the upper rooms, and to their surprise the senior rooster flew out from behind his office door, very embarrassed. He was wearing his flashy new trainers and a dazzling Rolex watch.

"There's the evidence that he was bribed at the Gift Factory when this church's robot was captured in Dry Valley," commented Pablo, very sad indeed that naughty Nick had sold out on the Master and made friends with Vermont.

Devine took Nikey Nick to one side to challenge him privately and warned him that if he didn't change then the matter would be discussed in front of everyone in the Mum City church.

"Ta rah a bit!" yelled Delilah before Devine had a chance to finish. This colourful chick did not show Devine the slightest sign of respect. Being a true Pretender, the fancy chick cuddled up to Nikey Nick and slammed the office door closed with a loud crash.

Devine left a copy of the letter from Blazing Glory with the secretary who was busy filing her claws at her desk. The

words of the letter were the same as those in the following Bible passage:

Revelation chapter 2 verses 12 to 17

Horrified, the Preps left the Mum City church and went back to Manna Farm for the rest of the day.

"Nikey Nick really had egg on his face, don't you think?" laughed Oscar. While it was clever of Oscar to pick up on these things, it was not something to be smug about. A feather drifted over from the chicken range to quietly correct the ever-learning Prep. He looked up the following words in his Bible and was challenged by what he read:

1 Corinthians chapter 13

Fortunately, all was not lost in Mum City and Devine was really impressed with the hens on the farm. As he and the other high flyers were served with some fresh bread and a helping of scrambled eggs, he observed how the chickens here were no great superstars but they were quietly attending to the finer details of serving the Master. And Devine gave a loud sigh of relief, too, when he saw that the mother hens were doing a great job of instructing the little chicks about the right way to Blazing Glory, by spending lots of time teaching them from the Bible.

Even though it had been a difficult and moving day, Devine knew that even if Nikey Nick refused to change, there would still be this faithful group of Preps left at Manna Farm. Devine decided to keep this as a thought for himself as 'Mum's the word' when you're on secret missions!

8
Belle of the Ball

It was time for the Preps to leave Manna Farm as it was critical they delivered the next letter and there was no time to spare. Before they took off, they exchanged wing-hugs with their new friends at the half-way house and encouraged one another along the way.

"Where are we going next?" enquired excitable Penny. She had not travelled to so many interesting places before.

Devine turned and looked at all three Preps, his eyes blazing with fire.

"We have a severe problem at the Thyatira City church," said Devine, pausing as his heart began to ache with sadness.

"Thya . . . what . . . are . . . yah," said tongue-tied Penny.

"Hmm, let's use the code name 'Rara' for our next city," smiled Devine, trying to help the tongue-tied sparrow. "The church at Rara City has made huge progress and has grown incredibly in size. It's a very popular church and many hundreds of birds go there. On the surface, it seems very strong and successful, and the building has had some fancy extensions. The members like to show off about how brilliant they are. But this is just a cover up, and in reality Pretenders have clearly got in and are leading members in wrong ways. The members are thinking and feeling wrong things and this is making them sick. Something terrible must have happened to the robot stationed there to be affecting everyone like this. It's urgent that we go and find out what is causing the disease to spread throughout the whole body of the church."

"Gosh, it sounds like the robot at the Rara church definitely needs to be looked at," commented caring Penny.

Without any further ado, they took off in the direction of Rara City. Since he needed to get to there as a matter of emergency, Devine's beak began to glow with a bright-red light. He looked like a flying ambulance speeding through the sky. The Preps couldn't travel as quickly as Devine so he asked dependable Pablo to guide the youngsters to Rara City. Without a trace, Devine disappeared in a flash of bright light.

Pablo decided to take the coast road to this strong city. Unfortunately, what started off as a fine and sunny afternoon soon turned into a blustery one. The swirling winds howled around the flying birds. As Penny held tightly onto Oscar's wing feathers she noticed beneath them, how high the waves were lashing against the ships on the sea. She held up her magnifying glass to try and see the distressed ships a little more closely.

"Magnifying glasses are for close examination, Silly," giggled Oscar.

Feeling a bit stupid, Penny strained her little eyes and saw something pretty alarming. "Oh no, it can't be!" she choked. She had left her beak open for too long while staring at the picture on one of the ship's flags, and had swallowed some flies.

"Cough it up, Penny, and tell us what you saw," replied Oscar trying to keep steady in the blustery winds.

"It's a pirate ship!" said Penny gasping in fright.

It was obviously a pirate ship because of the scary skull and crossbones picture on the flag wafting in the wind. The ship had been sailing from the docks just by Vermont's Gift Factory and he was using it to traffic more wonky robot parts for his cunning plans. Oscar decided to fly over the ship and as he did he could see a bright-red and -blue parrot held onto the captain's shoulder by a set of small shiny chains.

As they got closer, the Preps looked and then looked again. At the same time both Penny and Oscar cried out, "It's Charlie!"

"Charlie? Charlie who?" repeated Pablo.

"Repetition becomes a problem when you get too close to parrots!" laughed Oscar.

Oscar told Pablo all about Charlie the parrot and how he

had decided to follow the Master and had become a Christian on their *Trick or Treat?* adventure.

Now Charlie was in trouble for talking to everyone about Jesus. He had been captured by the buzzards and put under house arrest by Bully Bear, the ship's captain.

"Ahoy, my ship enemies!" bellowed Bully Bear at the top of his lungs. He couldn't call those on board his ship 'mates' because this bully had no mates, only enemies!

Pablo had experienced the dangers of the sea on many occasions in the past when he had followed his Bible hero Paul on his various sea-faring adventures. He told the two watchful Preps how he and Paul had been shipwrecked many times on their travels. Penny and Oscar loved to be told stories, so they found a cloud to rest on while Pablo showed them in the Bible what had happened to Paul. They read the following verses with great excitement:

Acts chapter 27 & chapter 28 verses 1 to 9

As they reached the end of the story, the cloud they were sitting on began to bounce around in fury. A large gust of wind hurled the Preps upwards into the rainy skies. They then span around and began to fall at an alarming speed. They landed on the port side of the ship with a loud crash.

The ship 'enemies' did not hear the three 'mates' because the sea was so rough and noisy. With great force, like big wet fists, the waves bashed against the pirate ship. On top of the noise from the waves, Bully Bear was becoming more and more annoyed with Charlie because he kept on singing the same hymn over and over again.

"If you don't shut up I'll put my smelly sock in your beak!" bullied the angry bear.

This didn't silence the singing parrot but instead spurred him on to sing louder than before and repeat even more verses. After the hundredth time of hearing the same tune, Bully Bear roared in anger because he could take no more from the jolly bird.

"Roarrrrr!" yelled the bad-tempered bear.

"Gulp," whispered the hiding Preps.

Bully Bear's roar was louder than the crashing waves. He lifted up his long claws and loosed the chain attached to his shoulder and began to swing it around in the air. Unfortunately, Charlie's foot was still attached to the other end of the chain! Watching from the port side of the ship, the Preps began to pray for Charlie's safety.

With a loud growl, Bully Bear let go of the chain as Charlie was thrown up, up and up away into the air towards the raging sea. It was as if time stood still as Charlie drifted in slow motion into the windy sky. Miraculously, the winds seemed to be carrying him in the air above the raging seas.

As the Preps watched and prayed from the pirate ship, who should slide across the deck but Cyril the sulky snake. Pablo had faced such slippery dangers before, when he had been on the island of Malta with the apostle Paul, and he knew the snake couldn't harm him. The bald eagle very boldly showed the two young Preps some heroic actions. Quickly, he grabbed Cyril in his claws and flew off the deck, dropping the sulky snake directly onto Bully Bear's head.

"Splat!" sounded Cyril as he landed with a crash.

It was a nice, furry, soft landing for Cyril but an unexpected strike for Bully Bear. Cyril's sticky, slimy snakeskin left a gooey mess on the growling bear's fur. Having scored a direct hit on the spiteful enemy, Pablo then stretched out his mighty eagle wings and, as fast as the speed of light, swooped and caught Charlie just before he dropped into the sea.

"Hurray, he's saved!" cheered Oscar and Penny, who couldn't believe their eyes.

With a roar of praise to Father God they took off into the

rainy skies, leaving Bully Bear chasing Cyril around the deck in a rage.

Oscar and Penny followed Pablo and Charlie, who landed in an Olive Grove by the beach. They were thrilled to see Charlie who just couldn't stop talking about all the great things that had happened since he had decided to follow the Master and become a Christian. They all soaked themselves in the oil found in the Olive Grove as they expressed great delight at Charlie's miraculous escape. While the young Preps giggled away, Pablo was beginning to worry because it was getting late.

"It's time to say goodbye," interrupted Pablo.

"Oh dear, we must say 'ta ra' as we are needed in 'Rara' on a secret mission," said Penny to Charlie, still in a giggly mood.

The Preps promised to meet up with Charlie again one day but explained to him that right now they had to go and help Devine on a very important secret mission. Charlie was quite nosey and wanted to know more about what they were up to.

"What secret, what secret?" questioned the repetitive parrot.

"We can't talk about the mission just in case it endangers our safety, but you can pray for us that the Rara church listens to Devine," said Penny, accidentally giving a bit too much top secret information to Charlie.

"'Rara' church?" repeated Charlie. "Where's the 'Rara' church?"

This was the code name for the church and so fortunately Charlie was none the wiser. Without giving away any more information they gave Charlie a 'holy' peck on both cheeks –

as he liked everything twice, especially kisses – and took off into the showery sky.

Pablo took a sharp right-turn from the coast road and flew the Preps over some strange-looking fields.

"The menacing mist must rest heavily in this area," commented Oscar, noticing the dead fields.

However, it wasn't so much the mist that had damaged the fields but the poisonous red field in the centre of the landscape that had leaked its poison into the surrounding ground.

"This is called the 'Field of Blood'," declared Pablo. "Judas, one of Jesus's disciples, betrayed Jesus with a kiss. He handed Jesus over to his enemies, selling him to them for thirty pieces of silver, to be put to death on the cross. In the end, Judas was so troubled by what he had done, that he died. This field was bought with the money that he swapped for his friendship. No-one has ever lived on this land and nothing can grow on it either," concluded Pablo.

With a little help from Pablo, the Preps checked the story in their Bibles and found it to be true.

Matthew chapter 26 verses 47 to 50

"My goodness," sighed Penny, as they landed near the field just by the Rara church. She couldn't understand how anyone could betray such a loyal friend as Jesus.

Surprisingly, the land leading up to the Rara church had been closed off. Colourful tape had been wrapped around the fences so that nothing or no-one could enter it. Stretching all around the edge of the field was a long line of birds. There were all different kinds of species but one thing they had in common was that they were very sick. The sick birds had all formed a queue, and at the front the Preps caught sight of Devine. The birds were all waiting to be touched by Devine's healing wings, as he had the power to make them well again. In a frantic dash, the Preps flew to the front of the line to ask Devine if there was anything they could do to help. Devine was glad to see his friends and told them of his findings at the Rara church.

"The members of this church have become sick. Their leader, Bella the sparrowhawk – distantly related to the buzzards – is really a Pretender. Trickery must run in her blood because she is so similar to Vermont's helpers, the buzzards," declared Devine. "She has been given time to change but she continues to lead the other members of the church in wrong ways, also known as 'sin'. This sin has had an ill effect on her and those who follow her wrong teaching. You must be really careful, especially because her closest friend and advisor is the Night Wolf."

Penny gasped with fright because she could clearly remember the Night Wolf's luminous eyes glowing in the dark woods when she had met him on her previous *Trick or Treat?* journey.

Devine gave Penny time to catch her breath as he continued to explain the dangers at the Rara church. "Bella is a beautiful bird with silky, strong feathers. She is described by the watching crowd as the 'belle of the ball'. Bella uses her beauty to mesmerise the audience, and with her charm she manages to keep away any real challenge from those who don't like her," explained Devine as he continued to heal the sick birds that stood in line. "Bella had a bad attitude and her circus-like performances at the church have led the audience into bad ways. Those attending the church like to be entertained and have forgotten how to worship Father God in a true way. There are always plenty of clowns performing to keep the crowd of birds happy, but even this doesn't work when they become sick. However, Father God sees everything, even when wrong ways are covered over by a big cloak," warned Devine. "Nothing misses his attention."

The Preps decided it was time to go and inspect the Rara robot, so they waved goodbye to Devine and, covering their beaks with one wing to avoid infection, they flew off in an awkward manner, each flapping wildly with their one free wing. Once inside the church, they looked for clues as to where the robot might be hiding. Some loud, thumping music was blaring out from a glass-sided room located up on the balcony. They looked at each other, nodded, and hopped up a flight of steps to the sound room, where the noisy music was coming from.

Their suspicions about the robot's location were right and, as they entered the room, they caught sight of a strong, towering robot in the corner, looking a bit like a bodybuilder and flexing its strong muscles. They couldn't go too near the robot due to the infection it was spreading, so they tried to examine it from a distance. On the surface, it looked like a fit, healthy robot. The robot was clothed in a bright-red, -white and -blue cloak. The cloak had a large collar, and a wide skirt hanging over the feet, which looked a bit like a brightly coloured circus tent. It was a clever way of hiding the robot's sick body.

"When this robot was captured by the buzzards in Dry Valley it appeared to escape without any noticeable damage, and none of the body parts were removed in the Gift

Factory. Sadly, though, damage has occurred on the inside of the robot and it is spreading like a vicious disease through all the body parts," explained Pablo, aware of the fact that Devine wasn't with them to offer his expert knowledge, so he needed to be extra sharp to correctly diagnose the problem. He continued, "Vermont was cunning and decided to keep the problem hidden, which is why the robot is wearing the brightly coloured skirt that looks like a circus tent. He also sprayed the inside of the robot with a thick coating of his toxic mist. LuSINda the toothless lion then filled the robot's teeth with gold. This gold didn't set properly and seeps into the rest of the robot, making its body sick. Bella likes the gold teeth and refuses to remove them. The disease is spreading from the robot and making all the church members ill, too. It's a terrible situation."

"Look at how the whole robot has turned a sickly yellow colour," noticed Penny.

"Can you see the nasty yellow pus seeping through the joints of the robot, staining its cloak?" added Oscar, staring at the sight which was beginning to make him feel a little bit icky sick too.

"Let me see, let me see," repeated Penny whose eyesight was not as sharp as an eagle's. "The gold from the teeth has caused the sickly stains."

"It's such a shame," said Pablo, sadly, "because in spite of the worsening condition of the robot and the church members, Bella refuses to say sorry and change. Her stubborn ways have now taken her to a sick-nest and she is in urgent need of 'tweetment'. However, the local bird doctors can't help her because she needs to help herself and repent of her wicked ways."

It was time to go back and join Devine, so the three detective birds left the sound room and the sickly robot and headed back outside. Staring at the long queue of sick birds, the Preps wondered if there was any hope for the Rara church members.

As they prayed and gave their worries to Father God, a feather rested at their feet. They lifted up their heads in hope as they read the following words in their Bibles:

Psalm 25 verse 14

Pablo then shouted out these words loudly to the crowd so that everyone could hear. He continued, trembling as he spoke, "Father God will reveal his secrets to those who show him respect. He will make an agreement with all those of you who are ready to do this so that you can be safe from catching the disease." Finally, he instructed all those who were ready to respect Father God to meet in the Olive Grove just outside the city gate.

Later that night, many loyal birds turned up, hoping to become Preps. They were sick and tired of pretending. The oil from the olive trees overflowed as Father God gave each Prep the power to win and continue along the right way until the Master's return. The oil acted as medicine and made them well.

It was getting late and Oscar and Penny were becoming tired. Caringly, Pablo tucked them up safely in one of his mobile nests in the Olive Grove. When they were settled, he continued to help the crowd of birds that had come for prayer.

Then Devine left Pablo in charge of the birds as he flew

over the Rara church, sprinkling it and the surrounding land with pure white snow. The snow would freeze which meant that the spread of infection would stop for a time. By doing this, Devine was offering Bella a chance to change.

In the flurry of snowflakes, he dropped the important letter for Bella to read so that she could clearly see the warning. Bella watched the pure-white falling snow from her sick-nest which was up in the church rafters. This plush penthouse nest had become her private hospital room. The letter was carried by a gentle breeze and floated through a crack in a stained glass window and landed on her bed. She thought the letter may be a get well message from her followers.

When she opened it, Bella was clearly not a happy bird. The letter contained the following verses from the Bible:

Revelation chapter 2 verses 18 to 29

Time would tell, as the Last Hour was drawing to a close, whether Bella would listen and have a change of heart.

With Devine in flight, delivering his important message from Blazing Glory to Bella, Pablo decided to dismiss the crowd of birds. It was time for him to rest from the demanding day. First, though, he prayed for this needy group of Preps because he was moved with compassion for them.

His prayers were carried across the secret winds to Devine who sent a special instruction back to him to help the sick friends. Hearing Devine's instruction, Pablo asked a member from the Rara church, Lydia, a tiny starling, to bring a large supply of cotton hankies to the Olive Grove from her nest. Lydia loved Jesus and she showed this love by serving her community. She worked hard, making purple fabric to earn a living. Without hesitation, she flew over to Pablo with her family and friends, bringing hundreds of small, square, purple hankies.

Disturbed by all the coming and going and with so much to do, Penny and Oscar jumped up out of their mobile nest. They began helping Pablo and set to work soaking each hanky in oil. Pablo then prayed a prayer of healing over the hankies.

"Place a hanky on the head of any bird who becomes sick and they will be made well as you pray," Pablo instructed the Preps at the Rara church.

As he finished addressing the crowd, a bright light lit up the dark night sky. It was Devine. Electrified with power from Blazing Glory, he descended, clasped the hankies in his claws and then distributed one to each of the many Preps.

"What an unusual end to the day," thought Penny as the crowd of birds left, waving their oily purple hankies.

With the  Olive Grove now quiet, the two young friends padded their nest with some of the spare oily hankies. The nest was so bright and comfortable that it made Penny and Oscar glow with contentment. After Pablo had settled down to sleep, things were no longer quiet. His snoring was loud and boring.

"What shall we do?" sobbed tired little Penny who was desperate for a good night's sleep.

"I know," replied Oscar, picking up a spare oiled hanky. He flew over to Pablo's nest and placed the hanky over his beak in the hope that it would cure his snoring!

"Ah, ah, alleluia!" responded Penny as she snuggled down to sleep in complete silence.

9
Spots

It was soon time for the young Preps to rise and shine but they were all very sleepy because of their late night. Curiously, a magpie was flying in circles around the Olive Grove. The magpie's attention had been caught by the brightly coloured hankies in the Preps' nest.

"How pretty," commented Maggie the magpie, who loved taking things which did not belong to her.

Like a bolt of lightning, she struck like a thief in the night. In a flash, Maggie swooped down and snatched the purple cloths from Penny and Oscar's nest, right from under their sleeping beaks! It was such a surprise that they both sat bolt upright and bumped heads.

"Ouch!" squealed the two friends together in perfect harmony. "We've been robbed, help!" they began to cry.

Before they had time to dry their tears, Pablo flew over in a startled rush to see what the commotion was about.

"What's up, birdies?" asked Pablo, very concerned.

"A thief came and stole our hankies," sobbed little Penny who was unable to wipe her little beak because, of course, she had no hanky!

Before she had time to finish the tale, in flew Devine with

a hanky for both the startled young Preps. This hanky was pure white because Devine had carried it from Blazing Glory. He always carried a supply of white hankies in his pure white feathers because comforting those who were sad was one of his main tasks. He wasn't troubled by the theft as it only served to confirm the importance of their next flight.

"That is just like the warning we are to take to the next church in Sardis," declared Devine.

"What do you mean?" asked Oscar.

"Hmm," said Pablo, as he already knew what was coming. Having studied at the High Flyers Academy, and being such an expert scholar, Pablo knew much of the Bible off by heart.

Devine showed the Preps the following letter in their Bibles, and they read the words in a hurry:

Revelation chapter 3 verses 1 to 6

Oscar began to chuckle. The laughter was catching and the rest of the birds began to laugh too. Before long, the whole of the Olive Grove roared with laughter. As they laughed, the birds were all soaked with an extra helping of oil for the day.

After a few big deep breaths, Oscar managed to compose himself and let the others in on the joke. "Sardis is such a funny name," smirked Oscar. "I've thought of a great code name for this church and it's . . . wait for it. . ."

"Come on," tittered Penny.

"Sardines!" laughed Oscar, finding the fishy connection very amusing. Eagles love fish.

Pablo found this so funny that he fell off the branch and bumped his bald head as he hit the ground. There wasn't too much damage, just a huge red lump which began to grow like a big, round golf ball on top of his head. Speedy Penny flew straight across to help old Pablo and landed on his head to stroke his wound.

"Ouch!" yelled Pablo as he brushed Penny off the throbbing lump on his head.

"Woops, sorry," responded Penny as she stared at the 'gentleness' badge on her wing feathers. "I must learn not to be quite so clumsy when caring for others."

"This is turning out to be quite a morning," chuckled Devine. "Spotty lumps are also part of this next church's problem, which from now on we will refer to as 'Sardines'!"

The Preps all scratched their heads, wondering what all this meant. Pablo didn't scratch his for long because it was quite sore with the huge lump that was now pounding. Devine prayed for them all to remain safe during the day ahead, and he also prayed for Pablo's headache to go away. Then they all took off, filled with great joy at the thought of their continuing adventure.

They flew through the hazy skies at a steady pace. It was very foggy because of the menacing mist around Sardines City. Quickly, they flew into the sleepy city, looking out for the Sardines church. Interestingly, there was a strong, fishy smell in the air which seemed to be rising from the church just coming in to view.

"Phew, what's that smell?" commented Penny as she tried to hold her breath.

Overwhelmed by the pong, they landed in the parking zone near the church because they needed to use their wings to hold their beaks. Trying to keep out the smell, the Preps tried to speak to each another still holding their beaks but couldn't understand one another properly. Struggling not to breathe in the fishy air too much, they headed into the church through the main door, where a church service was going on.

"Phew!" cried Penny over and over again.

"Cor dear!" responded Oscar as he began to turn a peculiar green colour.

Pablo said nothing as he didn't want to breathe in the horrid smell.

"'Sardines' is a good name to describe this place," whispered Devine, placing his wing over his beak. "The members are all packed in like sardines and cannot move. It seems as if they are being trained to stay in the building

instead of going out on mission with the Good News about Jesus. It looks like a successful place because it's so big and tightly packed but the disgusting smell tells a different story."

The Preps turned their beaks towards the high open door at the back of the church to take in a big breath of cleaner air. Curiously, they caught sight of hundreds of pure white doves hovering above the building. These doves behaved differently from the other member birds that flew into the building. They were the freedom flyers of the Sardines church. They loved the Master and were looking for his return. They wore white, just like it said in the letter the Preps had read earlier, and each dove's name was written in Father God's special book in Blazing Glory.

It was time to go in search of the wonky robot to find out what was causing the dreadful stink. Quick-thinking Penny, after a good peer around the place, noticed a sign above a door reading 'Church Kitchen'. Putting two and two together, she whispered loudly to the others, "Hey, follow me. I wouldn't be at all surprised if the robot is hiding in the kitchen. It's where you would store and prepare fish, after all. Let's go and have a look together."

Penny's gut feeling was right. There, standing next to the oven was a stocky, square robot. All the body parts seemed to be in the right place but the terrible smell told a thousand stories. Devine and the keen birdwatchers began looking a little more closely at the robot's body.

"It appears that this robot was damaged when it was attacked by Vermont as it left Dry Valley," said Devine. "If you look closely you will notice that it has a skin problem. It's covered with lots of different kinds of spots!"

"You could play a game of Dot-to-Dot with this lot of spots," remarked sharp Oscar.

The Preps got out their magnifying glasses and examined the outside of the robot. It had a massive outbreak of lots of different types of spots. Some were large brown freckles while other spots were red with a sticky yellow head on top.

"Yuck, that's gross!" said Penny, who felt a little off-colour looking at the sticky, spotty mess.

The most dangerous spots were those that lay beneath the skin. They were blind spots and were usually difficult to recognise and very painful to touch.

Oscar got out his mobile phone so that he could examine the blueprint photos that he had taken back in Vermont's office at the Gift Factory. On the plans were written some of the ingredients which had been put into the menacing mist. Too much exposure to the mist would bring out this spotty disease on the robot's body. Devine explained from the plans that the large brown freckles were called age spots. They were a sign of moth-eaten metal.

"What's moth-eaten metal?" asked Pablo, who didn't often give much care to his own complexion.

"This spotty condition has happened because the older members in the church have been exposed to the mist. Even though they are older, and should be mature, they are not passing on their wisdom to the younger church members to help them to understand how to protect themselves from the harmful mist," said Dr. Devine. "Simple obedience to the Master's teaching in the Bible would have prevented the damage. Unfortunately, those attending this church have become set in their ways. They hear what Jesus says in the Bible but they never put his words into action. This is causing the formation of age spots," summed up Devine, giving his verdict on the spotty mess.

"Well, what are *these* sticky spots?" asked Penny as she touched the sticky goo with her wing-tip. "Yuck!" she squealed, sneakily wiping the mess off down the feathers on Oscar's back.

Devine coughed as he noticed her cheeky act and handed her another white hanky to remove the goo from Oscar's back.

"The red lumps with yellow heads are quite easy to diagnose," answered Dr. Devine. "They are teenage spots."

Hearing this, Oscar went bright red. His cheeks burned with embarrassment because he had begun to develop a cluster of teenage spots just above his young beak, but his good friends were kind and turned a blind eye to them. Seeing Oscar blushing, Devine swiftly turned the attention away from the spots on his beak.

Devine went on to explain that the young members of the church were behaving badly and had become out of control. "This has caused the outbreak of immature spots on the robot's body," he said.

"Gasp!" cried Oscar and Penny. "How did this happen and can it be treated?"

"This young spotty problem is not down to having a shortage of good speakers to teach the younger ones, because there are plenty of members here that can teach well. But not many older members are prepared to become like fathers in being responsible for the growth and development of the young birds. Sadly, they give in to what the young birds want, allowing behaviour that is not acceptable in Blazing Glory," summed up Devine.

Pablo was very familiar with this problem as he had dealt with a similar spot of trouble before, during his training days. He showed the young Preps some words from their Bibles that the apostle Paul had written to another church:

1 Corinthians chapter 4 verse 15

Devine then went on to talk about the blind spots. "These spots lie beneath the surface and are not seen. Many church members spend most of their time pointing out faults in others but they forget their own faults," he said, before going on to quote the following well-known words spoken by Jesus:

Matthew chapter 7 verses 1 to 5

"When problems are ignored, they become painful to touch. If any other body part touches on that problem or bad attitude, the other body part will react in an angry way," concluded Devine.

"Shocking!" remarked Oscar.

"What's even more shocking is that this 'Sardines' body thinks it is doing well but the smell tells us it's a dying church," responded Devine. "Just look at how the robot's eyelids have been rolled down like the shutters on a sardine tin. Sadly, this shows that the church members have stopped looking out at the world of need around them and just keep looking inwards," concluded Devine, speaking his final word on the whole spotty, dotty matter.

It was time to leave the kitchen and head back outside. Drifting in on the horizon, the mist began its daily attack on

Sardines City. Devine flew with the Preps onto the roof of the church building where they were greeted excitedly by the pure white doves. They looked remarkably like Devine.

The doves were watching and  praying on the roof because they had become more and more worried about the behaviour of their leader Chip the woodpecker and his followers. Chip loved to chip away at all the dead wood found inside the church building. He was an expert 'chippy'. His constant tap, tap, tapping at the church members had worn them down so much that they hardly did anything any more.

"Hardly anything of great value, that is," complained the frustrated doves.

Chip, however, did keep the members busy. They were required to attend church every day of the week. This left them no time for friendship with other birds living in nearby tree tops.

The doves had just finished telling the Preps about their difficulties when the other birds began to arrive at the church in droves to attend the next service. Strangely, their heads were hung low and they all looked sad and tired. Devine wanted to check out if there were any Pretenders in the church before he spoke to Chip about his concerns.

The pure white doves led the Preps back into the church through a skylight in the roof, where they settled on some old, rotten wooden beams. Here they could get a bird's-eye view of what was taking place.

"What's that noise, tap, tap, tapping?" whispered Oscar.

"It's the woodpeckers counting in the members as they come through the door," answered Pablo.

"Why do they do that? They're chipping away at the wood around the entrance," noticed Penny.

"It's one of those common problems which happen when a big church brags about how it has more members and better facilities than the churches in the next city. Sadly, doing this puts a limit on what Father God can do. God is far more concerned about the well-being of the members than how many of them there are," summed up Devine.

"If only they could all see the bigger picture," said the wise bald eagle Pablo.

"They would if they opened the shutters covering the wonky robot's eyes," replied smart Oscar.

Within seconds of the birds taking their perches inside the church, Chip began his repetitive tap, tap, tapping with his beak. He began telling the members that they were not doing enough. This only made matters worse because more and more spots then began to appear on the wonky robot's body.

Devine searched around the inside of the church with his fiery eyes. He wondered where the young fledglings were. The doves informed him that there were no perches for the little ones, so they had their own special room. Besides, Chip said they made too much noise during his bird-tapping speeches.

"The children have a special visitor today. He's meant to be a great entertainer and this tends to keep the little ones quiet," said one of the doves, a little concerned.

"Out of sight, out of mind," thought the Preps, all at the same time.

Devine was very worried about the younger birds, so he asked one of the doves to take him and the Preps to the room where they met. They flew into a cramped room at the back of the church building and were surprised at the loud din that met them. It was a very noisy group. Some of the shy little birds didn't like all the commotion but this didn't seem to matter as most of the others had got used to it.

They found a place to perch on a high ledge at the back of the room. Unexpectedly, there was a loud drum roll. This week's special guest was getting ready to entertain the sweet little birdies. Suddenly there was a puff of smoke – which looked a little too much like Vermont's menacing mist – and the guest entertainer appeared with a flash of light.

"I wonder who it could be?" piped up Penny, keeping her eyes fixed towards the front stage. "Oh no!" she cried as she swallowed a big gulp of mist.

To their horror, it was Wiz the lying lizard. Speechless, the Preps didn't know what to say and almost fell off their perch. Worryingly, the young birds didn't seem too bothered because they loved to watch tricks, and the big birds thought it was just harmless fun. Devine knew differently and didn't wait a moment to act. He took off, and with great speed flew down and snatched the magic wand out of the lizard's claws. With no magic power now that he didn't have his wand, Wiz stood very still.

"Boo!" cried all the little sparrows, beginning to get restless.

Realising he was powerless, Wiz slipped out of the side door and didn't bother collecting his fee. The big birds taking care of the little sparrows didn't know what to do. At this point, the three Preps rose to the occasion. Escorted by the fine white doves, they flew onto the stage. Pablo thought this was a good time to tell the little sparrows a Bible story. Penny and Oscar performed a drama to help colour the tale. The little sparrows loved to hear stories, especially true ones.

Devine handed each of the little sparrows their own Bible and magnifying glass so that they could learn to be Preps. They flapped around in excitement as they scurried through the pages of their Bibles to:

Acts chapter 16 verses 9 to 40

This may have been a long read for some, but the exciting way in which Pablo told the true tale of the apostle Paul's time working for the Master meant that the young crowd stayed focused and happy. Perhaps this also had something to do with Devine being present? In fact, you could have heard a feather drop as they perched there, enjoying listening to the wisdom of old, bald Pablo. Pablo was not just a good teacher. By his kindness, he also showed the little sparrows what the heart of a caring father looks like.

Penny, being a fine example of a good Christian sparrow, then prayed for all the little sparrows. They were happy as they had tasted something quite different that day. They had seen that Father God's great power is far bigger and better than the power found in a Pretender like Wiz. All the little sparrows cheered and flapped as they clapped their wings in praise to Father God.

It wasn't long before Chip heard about what was happening with the little sparrows and he was tapping mad.

"Tap, tap, tappety, TAP!" yelled the annoyed woodpecker.

He called for Devine and the Preps to come to his office immediately. Unafraid of his tapping threats, they said goodbye to the little sparrows first and left them in the care of the pure white doves, who could be trusted to lead them in the right way. The doves invited the little sparrows on a special outing to the nearest Olive Grove in Dove County. All the sparrows wanted to be part of this great day out, even the shy, quiet ones.

When Devine and the Preps arrived at Chip's office they were quite surprised. They were going to knock on the door but found that all the wood had been chipped away and there was no door to knock on! Pablo gave a loud cough and they entered the office. It was very tatty because of all the dead wood on the inside of the church building.

Chip had been tapping so hard, waiting for the Preps, that his beak had got stuck in the dead wood on his desk. All three Preps had to assist in pulling his beak out.

"Kerplunk!" sounded Chip's beak as it broke free from the splintering wood.

Devine then spoke to Chip in a firm but loving manner, asking him to consider the contents of the special letter sent from Blazing Glory. He advised Chip to wake up and see all the dead wood before it was too late. The day for the Master's return was fast approaching and there wasn't much time left.

"If you don't change your ways, Chip, your name will be chipped out of the Book of Life in Blazing Glory," warned Devine.

"What must I do to change?" asked Chip who was getting so nervous that he couldn't stop tapping his desk.

Devine took Chip up and out of the building through the skylight to where the doves loved to pray. Sitting on the church roof, they watched the menacing mist creeping around the city. Flying high as freedom flyers, the doves circled the city. It was a powerful picture for Chip to see. Caringly, Devine encouraged Chip because there was still hope if he would just look beyond the walls of the Sardines church building.

He then flew back inside and took Chip to see the wonky robot in the kitchen. He pointed out all the spots to Chip and explained the reasons why they had appeared on the robot.

"Gosh, there are so many spots you could play Dot-to-Dot," chipped in the woodpecker, repeating what Oscar had said earlier.

Chip then asked if he could be left alone with the letter so that he could read it and decide what to do. With so many spotty problems to treat on the robot and all the dead wood and splinters inside the church building, Chip sighed a big sigh because he was unsure if he had enough time to get things right. He tapped away on the shutters which covered the robot's eyes, trying to think of whom he could blame for the spotty mess. Sadly, he had his own blind spots and could not see his own need to change first.

There were still greater works to be done before the Master's return so, with haste, Devine called the Preps and they said goodbye to tapping Chip, before heading back into the main church building and leaving through the skylight. As they left, they wondered if Chip would listen to the alarm bell ringing through the words of the letter from Blazing Glory.

"Jesus, the Master, will one day return for his Church but only for those who are awake and watching for his coming. We can pray that the letter from Blazing Glory will act like a mirror so that Chip will recognise his need to change," said Devine as they took off to continue with their mission.

10
Tiny Tim

The Preps flew onwards and upwards, a little dazed from all the distressing events at the Sardines church. They were especially glad to get away from the strong, fishy smell.

Unfortunately, as Oscar had taken off in such a hurry, a small splinter had got stuck in his claw from the dead wood on the rotting church roof rafters.

"Ouch!" cried Oscar as he tried to stay in flight.

"What's going down, bro?" asked Penny as she gripped onto his wing feathers more tightly after the bumpy take off.

"I've got a splinter in my claw from the dead wood in the Sardines church," sniffled Oscar who was clearly distressed by his injury.

Pablo could see all the commotion and was instructed by Devine to go and help the young Preps. He swooped like a true eagle beneath Oscar and used his back like a landing pad for the injured bird to rest on. Oscar peered through his bent glasses and caught the wind thermal above Pablo, who then rose up to catch him and his frightened passenger Penny. They touched down with a slight jolt but were both safe and sound on the great bald eagle's back. Being a caring friend, kind Penny climbed off Oscar's back, clutching on tightly to his feathers with her claws and then hanging onto his ankle. She found the sharp splinter lodged in his claw, pulled it out with her tiny beak and spat it out gracefully over the side. The spit carrying the splinter flew through the air and hit an enemy buzzard in the eye. The crafty buzzard had been following the Preps, but not any more!

"Yikes!" shrieked the buzzard as he cried out to the other buzzards on the ground for permission to land. Unable to see, he crashed into a tall oak tree and went hurtling to the ground.

Meanwhile, unaware of the buzzard's attack and defeat, Penny gently patted Oscar's claw and climbed up onto his back. Then Pablo decided he would carry the two friends to their next destination so that Oscar could recover from his trauma. He prayed for Father God's peace on board their flight, and for the way to be made safe and open for their continued mission.

The birds were feeling hungry and there was no food on board the flight. They were unable to land for refreshments because the menacing mist over Sardines was very, very thick as they left. Devine wasn't too worried about their hunger because he knew fresh bread would await them at their destination, Philadelphia, home of the next church.

Pablo tried to let his young crew know where they were going. "Philly. . .," stuttered Pablo, "we're flying to Philly . . . dilly."

"Chilly?" responded Penny. "Yes, it is quite chilly up here."

"No! Philly, Silly," tried Pablo again. Once again, this long name was difficult to pronounce, especially as Pablo wore false teeth.

Devine immediately came to the rescue, sending a message across the secret winds that this city would be known as 'Deli'. It was the home of the 'Faithful' church, so they knew a fresh bite to eat would be found in Deli.

The creeping mist was becoming thicker and thicker on the ground beneath the freedom flyers. The Preps began to pray again and, as they did so, the lights in the tube pots on their wings began to burn brightly, lighting up their way.

"I wonder why the mist is so thick?" asked Oscar.

"It's because the church in Deli is strong and faithful to the Master, Jesus. Every time Vermont tries to send in an extra supply of menacing mist, the light inside the church building pushes the dark mist back out of the city. This has created a big black wall around the outside of the city, and it's hard for us to break through it from this side," replied Pablo.

Pablo, being an older Prep, not only had false teeth but fading eyesight too. The thick mist gave him poor visibility as they approached the city of Deli. It was hard for him to see, even with the light on board the flight glowing from the edge of the Preps' wing feathers. His difficulties were known as 'a thorn in his side' but they did not make him complain or become bitter. He had experienced obstacles to his work on many occasions in the past, and he knew that Devine would make a way.

He was right. Devine used the letter from Blazing Glory that he was taking to Deli as his anti-mist clearing device. He read the words from the letter out loud, with the Preps reading them in their Bibles as they travelled on Pablo's steady back.

Revelation chapter 3 verses 7 to 13

"Open!" shouted Oscar and Penny together in excitement.

This was a nice easy word found in the letter, which told them clearly that whenever Father God opens a door, nothing or no-one can shut it. Therefore, as they were carrying out Father God's work, they knew and trusted that he could do anything. Nothing or no-one is more powerful than God's word.

A dazzling feather cut through the thick mist as it pierced through the darkness. Oscar reached up and grabbed it in his beak.

Zechariah chapter 4 verse 6

Together, they boldly read the words out loud and as they did, the dark mist was pushed back like two curtains being opened right before their eyes. A blaze of light came flooding through and reflected on each of Devine's brilliant white feathers. This was as a dazzling display of Father God's great power. The light spectacle commanded an air of respect in the skies and the Preps were speechless. Strangely, as the birds flew into the light there was a huge roar of wings flapping on the ground. The noise whirled around in the sky and continued upwards towards Blazing Glory. The Preps had come into the open heaven directly above Deli and were being lifted upwards by sounds of worship being sent from the church members to Father God. All the hunger and tiredness from the journey just seemed to disappear into the dark mist they had left behind.

With a clear runway ahead of him, Devine began the descent and landed at the foot of the Deli church, followed by the three Preps.

Pablo was itching to go inside the enormous church as the next meeting was due to start very soon. As they tiptoed into the building, Oscar wondered why everything seemed so quiet. There was a powerful hush in the room.

"Who's in charge here? I can't see," said little Penny quietly as they flew forwards above the kneeling crowd of birds.

"You will struggle to see Tiny Tim the blue tit, the leader of this church," whispered Devine, "because he is very humble and he never stands in the way of the members praising Jesus. He leads this body of friends with great strength. Father God honours this strength of character which is known as 'humility'."

The young Preps were familiar with this word. It meant that someone was modest and didn't think too much of themselves, putting God and others first. They had learnt about it in one of their lessons at the Camp of Life Academy and they had each earned a fruit badge of humility on their first adventure along the way.

They followed Devine, who hovered over the gathered birds and gently brushed their bowed heads with the tips of his wings. Pablo shone with pride as he caught sight of his much-loved friend, Tiny Tim. He was kneeling in  prayer at the front of the church The Preps landed with Devine right next to Tiny Tim and immediately took to this fine little bird. After hugging his guests, Tiny Tim quickly stepped back and put Devine in the spot-light so that he could read the letter from Blazing Glory to the listening crowd.

The room was full of little swifts who cheered loudly as they heard the news that the Master, Jesus, was coming back soon. Devine struggled to get the birds to quieten down because they were so happy and encouraged by the news of the great day of Jesus's return being so close.

The swifts had little physical strength because they were so slender and small but they were strong in character because they diligently followed and obeyed the teaching from their humble leader, Tiny Tim. He was a great teacher, not just because of his well-rehearsed speeches, but because he led by example and lived by everything he taught.

Devine continued to read out the letter, which explained how strength of character would be rewarded in Blazing Glory. The swifts heard how, in Blazing Glory, they would become like strong, decorated pillars inside Father God's home. The letter also promised that they would each receive a new and special name when they arrived in Blazing Glory, as a reward for all the good and faithful works they had done in Deli. This news sent the swifts flying around like crazy birds. There was ordered chaos everywhere. It was a spectacular sight that the Preps would always remember.

The commotion finally settled down, and there was an announcement that there would be a break of five minutes. Devine came over to Oscar and Penny and they asked him if he would take them to see the church's robot so they could find out what made this church so good. Devine knew they'd find this robot exactly where it should be so they headed straight for the boiler room at one side of the church.

Sure enough, there in front of them, in the middle of the room stood the robot, looking so alive and fit. As the birds looked, their beaks dropped in wonder because it was extremely tall. In fact, it was so tall that a hole had had to be cut in the roof and the robot towered up above into the sky. It had two long, lanky legs and two funny, knobbly knees. This made Penny giggle inside the giggle box in her tummy.

"Cor! Look at the long legs on this robot," admired the short little sparrow, who would have loved to have been a few centimetres taller.

However, in spite of being so tall, the robot was very, very skinny. So skinny that, although on first sight it had seemed fit and well, it actually looked weak in appearance. It had been attacked by Vermont and the buzzards as it came out of Dry Valley but it hadn't been defeated by the evil genius.

"How did it manage to win against Vermont and the buzzards?" asked bewildered Oscar.

"This robot may have little outward natural strength of its own but inside it is extraordinarily strong. This is a mirror reflection of the members here at this church. The members may be weak and small, but they know that they can always rely on Jesus's strength to help them in everything they do," responded Devine, guiding them to the following verse in their Bibles, which showed them what they should do to be strong in this way.

2 Corinthians chapter 12 verse 9

Devine, Oscar and Penny headed back into the main church building. They didn't want to be late for the next part of the service, and Devine flew quickly up to the front and stood next to Tiny Tim.

As Oscar and Penny made their way to their perches, Oscar smiled and said, "Everything seems to work as it should in this church. This is just what we have been looking for."

"I love this place," squealed Penny. "Do you think I can make my home nest here when our mission is finished?"

"We should ask Devine where he wants us to go. Now, ssshh!" said Oscar, "It's time to be quiet. Remember how to use self-control."

A very important part of their gathering time together was about to take place. Suddenly, a light, sweet mist filled the air. It was the smell of fresh bread that had been baked in the church kitchen. The kitchen was one of the busiest parts of the church. The members here spent a lot of time baking bread and feeding the poor and hungry birds in Deli.

"Ah! Yummy, yummy!" swooned the hungry Preps.

All their tummies began to rumble in anticipation of the feast. The loaves of fresh bread were placed at the front of the church while Tiny Tim stood to one side. Next, some cool red berry juice was poured into little bowls. Suddenly, the candle on the golden candlestick on the small platform at the front of the church came to light. Oscar and Penny wanted to dive in and eat straight away but Pablo held them back. He wrapped one large wing around Oscar and restrained Penny with his claw.

"Wait!" cried Pablo. "Remember your manners, please."

The young Preps needed to find out from their manuals what their manners should be for eating at this special occasion. Pablo smiled at their enthusiasm and thought about how best to teach them the right way to behave. He wracked his brains and remembered that his hero Paul had written a very important letter detailing this special meal to another church. So he helped the young birds by turning the pages of his Bible to the right place to show Oscar and Penny what to do. With their tummies rumbling even louder, they picked up their magnifying glasses and read the words of Paul's letter.

1 Corinthians chapter 11 verses 20 to 33

With a loud gulp, the Preps realised what a serious occasion this meal was, and how important it was to wait for one another. After a short pause, Devine broke and blessed the bread. As he did so, the swifts twittered their thanks of praise to Jesus for all that he had done for them.

It seemed like a lifetime but it was only a few moments until the special guests were invited to come and eat first. Oscar was very hungry and tucked into the bread. Penny gave him a polite nudge because he was eating rather a lot, especially as there were so many other birds in the church who also needed to eat.

"Manners, Oscar, remember your manners," whispered Penny, nibbling on her piece of bread.

Strangely enough, the supply of bread didn't seem to get any smaller and there was plenty for all, with some left over.

While they waited for the others to take part in the special meal, Devine went over and sat next to Oscar and Penny and quietly explained to them why the robot they'd just seen was so tall. "Tiny Tim always remains small so that the Master can be seen. So, because Jesus is focused on and lifted up as Lord and the only one to be worshipped, the robot's body has become tall and can be seen for miles. This is its unique attraction and this is the main reason for the great success of the Deli church. Jesus is the main attraction, there are no celebrities here. Tiny Tim never started counting the number of birds he has taught, so he hasn't become big-headed about how well the church is doing. Neither has he limited how much Father God can do in this city," said Devine.

The key for success was shown in the following Bible verse which Devine asked Oscar to read out loud during the feast of bread and red berry juice:

John chapter 12 verse 32

In other words, wherever Jesus is truly worshipped as Lord, then people will be saved.

The members of the Faithful church in Deli were very, very busy, but they were busy doing the right things in the right way. For example, they always produced good fresh bread. The unique recipe for the bread was given by the Master Chef in Blazing Glory. It was the Master's words of instruction that made the bread taste so good. The Preps were going to stay overnight just so that they could learn from this amazing church.

Pablo wanted to send word to Pedro the kingfisher that he could come along and see the great things that were happening in Deli.

"How can we contact Pedro to invite him to come and see what amazing things are taking place here?" asked Pablo. "He would be so happy and encouraged to see this terrific church where the members are all working together in such a good way. It is just how the body of Christ should be."

"Hmm, I've got just the ticket," responded quick-thinking Tiny Tim.

Tiny Tim sent two of his quickest swifts, who were also his close friends, to the I-Spy church. Before they left, he instructed them to invite Pedro to Deli and in his absence they should stay and encourage the church at I-Spy. The swifts took off as a pair of champion birds, ready to rise to the challenges they were about to face in I-Spy.

The Preps most definitely wanted to hang around for as long as possible in Deli, so they decided to sleep over with their new-found friends. Deli was full of wonderful Olive Groves, and the Preps had trouble choosing which one to spend the night in. They made their way down the main street of tall trees and through a small garden at the end of a line of olive trees. This was Tiny Tim's personal Olive Grove. It was modest in size but very well cared for. In the corner of the Olive Grove was a bag with the words 'Miracle-Gro' on the side. The Preps wanted to take a look inside the bright plastic grow bag.

They flew towards it and as they did, Tiny Tim called out, "Stop!"

But it was too late. Oscar and Penny had disturbed the small robin redbreast nesting with her young birds inside the bag, and she flew away in fright. This was Robina the robin, who had been widowed and left with her small family of baby robins. Tiny Tim had kindly invited her to nest in safety in his Olive Grove. Horrified that they had frightened Robina, the Preps stood still so that they didn't alarm the chicks asleep in the nest. Tiny Tim asked them all to step back and wait so that Robina would be able to fly back to her nest.

"Why is the nest inside the grow bag?" asked Penny.

"LuSINda the toothless lion attacked and broke up their own home, just on the outskirts of Deli. Roberto, Robina's husband, lost his life trying to defend the nest. LuSINda had been lurking around for an easy target to attack, and sadly it was the robins. It was a rare attack because Vermont and his Stalkers are usually unable to do much damage here in Deli itself because everyone is trained so well and knows how to resist them. And, fortunately, we don't have many Pretenders in Deli," said Tiny Tim. "Instead, the Stalkers lie in wait just outside the city gates. Sadly, this attack caused all the eggs to hatch before time, so the swifts living in the tree tops near the city gates rescued the family and brought them here. The baby robins needed special care and lots of warmth. They needed a miracle just to survive and that is exactly what has happened. They have grown well in this bag of good, warm soil. Robina and her family are well supported by the birds in the tree tops down this street. This is the kind of religion that is accepted in Blazing Glory."

The Preps raced to read about the true religion described in the following Bible verse:

James chapter 1 verse 27

These words confirmed that what Tiny Tim had just said was true.

Robina flew back to the grow bag now that she felt safe. The Preps left her in peace, and found an olive tree where they could rest their tired wings for the night.

It wasn't easy to sleep because Pablo was doing his best to keep the young Preps awake, yet again. Not with his snoring this time, but chatting with Tiny Tim about their exciting memories of the times they had spent watching the missionary journeys of their Bible heroes during their time at the High Flyers Academy. Their tales were packed with daring dangers and colourful drama. Oscar and Penny peered over the edge of their branch in the olive tree so that they could listen to the stories. As they lent over, the oil seeping through the branch caused them to slip and land on Pablo's head below.

They thought he would be very cross but neither Tiny Tim nor Pablo could stop laughing. Even Devine circled in the air, enjoying the hilarious sight.

"What's so funny?" asked confused Penny.

They struggled to get an answer as Pablo roared with laughter. The sleeping swifts were quick to join in on the fun and they darted across the grove to hear what all the commotion was about.

"Ha, ha," laughed Pablo, rolling around. "I can't believe what's just happened. You both falling out of that tree reminds Tiny Tim and me of something very similar that we saw happen to the apostle Paul. Look, let me show you the true story in the Bible."

But Pablo was unable to compose himself, so he asked Penny to read the tale from her Bible to the laughing audience.

Acts chapter 20 verses 7 to 12

The listening swifts struggled to hear Penny above all the giggles. But Penny couldn't understand what was so funny about someone falling from a window and hurting themselves. Then she realised that the amusing part was that Paul's speech was so longwinded that it had sent the man to sleep and that's why he fell. When Penny got to the end of the story and saw that the injured man was made better, she began to chuckle too.

While all the birds in the Olive Grove were slipping around on the flowing oil and falling over laughing at this funny story, who should slip into view but Pedro the kingfisher. Pedro was well-known in Deli for being a great kingfisher who had played a big part in helping many of the swifts come to know Jesus. Pedro landed to a warm welcome from everyone in Tiny Tim's Olive Grove, except Pablo the bald eagle who was a little stand-offish because he and Pedro sometimes had picky disagreements.

"What's all the laughter about?" asked Pedro.

Tiny Tim told him about the apostle Paul's long speech in the story and its deadly result, to which Pedro gave an unwelcome comment to Pablo.

"Pablo, you're just like the apostle Paul. Your speeches always go on too long, too!" said sharp Pedro.

Pablo didn't like his beak-digging comment.

"At least my speeches are educated and interesting," replied Pablo proudly, showing a side to him the Preps had not seen before. Even the great bald eagle needed to work on his fruits and Be-attitude stripes.

With this, Pedro flew away to one tree and Pablo flew away to another tree. No-one knew quite what to do. Devine landed in the middle of the trouble and called for order.

"Come back Pedro and come back Pablo," said Devine as he put his claw down on such nonsense. Pedro flew back and so did Pablo. They gave each other a wing-hug and decided to put aside their differences for the greater good of those around them. Devine asked all those in the gathering to rest now for the night and soak in some oil, as Preps must always have a full supply. Rest was very important if they were going to fly long and strong.

As the sun rose in the cloudy sky, the bright light caused Penny to blink her eyes. She rubbed them because she couldn't believe what she saw. The robot from Deli was peering over the Olive Grove. It had now grown so tall that it stretched up to the skies. The fluffy white clouds looked like white hair on the robot's head. The bright-blue sky matched the robot's vivid blue eyes.

"What's happening?" cried the little sparrow at this unexpected sight.

Oscar opened his eyes and put on his bent round glasses. He was speechless. Tiny Tim rushed to help his disturbed little guests as he began to explain how the church members in Deli, where this robot came from, served the Master, Jesus.

"This robot is able to move about freely because his joints have been well-oiled. You see, the Deli church members always have a good supply of oil because they spend time talking to Father God and reading their Bibles. All the robot's body parts are in the right places and working as they should. This is a sign that the members are doing the work of the Master in the correct way that he instructed. Throughout the whole week, everyone hops from tree top to tree top talking to others about the Master and Blazing Glory. Everyone works together, each playing their part in helping someone else in need. We make sure that there are no needs in the tree tops. If a need is found, then the rest of the church members share what they have. It means that no-one becomes more important than anyone else. We believe that everyone is equally important. This is a good example of the Church, the body of Christ, working correctly. We all need each other," spoke the tiny leader, Tim.

He then got them to look up the following verses in their Bibles, which gave them the blueprint for their community work:

Acts chapter 2 verses 44 to 47

Suddenly, a loud bird call came piercing through the skies. This was a call for the swifts to pray. They were very quick to respond to the clear sound. Rapidly, one of the swift watchmen flew into the Olive Grove to speak to Tiny Tim. He informed him of a casualty at the city gate. Before the swift had time to finish, Pedro the kingfisher was up, up and away. Pedro would always jump when he saw a need for help. He never stopped to think about the consequences.

Everyone quickly followed Devine out of the Olive Grove, just behind Pedro. They were on the alert for the danger of the menacing mist or Vermont's vile assistants, and were particularly concerned because the attack on the casualty, a starling, had happened just outside Deli's gates.

In the distance, the Preps could see the fallen starling. His wing was broken and so were his fragile legs. The poor victim was tired and hungry and he asked Pedro for some help when he landed next to him. In a weak voice, the starling explained that he had tried to make it through the dark mist to Deli but he had been attacked by the Night Wolf as he paused for a rest in a bush. It had been an easy mistake to make because the Night Wolf's eyes had shone a small amount of light onto the lost bird's flight path. Duped by the fake light, he was struck to the ground and left as dead. In the morning light, he could see the city gate and so had crawled through the dust towards it in search of help.

Pedro, now joined by a huge flock of Preps, reached down to the starling, placed his wing-tip on his head and prayed. "I don't have any fresh bread on me, but what I do have I give you. By the power of Jesus Christ, rise up and fly!" declared Pedro, believing that Jesus would make this young starling well.

In a split second, the starling was made well and flew up into the sky, flying loops around the watching crowd and chirping with great delight. As he did this, a dazzling feather fluttered to the ground. Written on it were the Bible verses of a similar bright and happy story for the Preps to look up and read.

Acts chapter 3 verses 1 to 10

After the celebration had quietened down, Tiny Tim called everyone to come and pray. Oscar and Penny couldn't believe their young eyes. It was a stunning sight. There was a flock of birds which stretched further than their eyes could see. Then they saw the tall, skinny robot marching towards the city gate. It breathed out a huge lungful of breath into the mist outside the city. Miraculously, the mist was pushed back at least another mile. The air smelt fresh and clear because everything in this robot was working as it should. After breathing out another big lungful of breath, the robot's cheeks radiated with a bright-red glow. It had 'slap cheek' which is a mild facial rash. This was a sign that the members of the Deli church always turned the other cheek whenever they were insulted, just like the Master instructed. They had become experts in not striking back but always following Father God's ways in everything they did, even when dealing with those who tried to hurt them.

"Don't you think we should take the freedom that is found at the Deli church to help those we meet on our final mission?" asked quick-thinking Oscar, who was very impressed with what he had seen of the Faithful church.

Devine paused, deep in thought, and then produced a bright, shining, gold set of keys and handed them to Tiny Tim.

"Father God has given you these keys along with this letter. They are to be used so that whatever you close on earth in prayer will be closed in heaven and whatever you open on earth in prayer will be opened in heaven," answered Devine. "In other words, when you pray you can expect what you pray to happen."

These powerful keys were given to the Faithful church in Deli and its members because they had proved to be faithful friends of the Master. The apostle Peter, Pedro's Bible hero, had been given similar keys by Jesus. Pedro pointed this fact out to the young Preps as they looked up the relevant verses up in their Bibles.

Matthew chapter 16 verse 19

Pedro the kingfisher remembered back to how he had seen the apostle Peter use the keys and how great things had happened in very difficult situations when he had prayed.

Tiny Tim took the keys and handed them to Mark, the blameless swift. Tiny Tim then suggested that he, Pedro and Pablo should fly together with Oscar and Penny, on the final quest. He was going to leave Mark in charge of Deli. He knew Mark could be trusted with the special keys and the running of the Deli church's daily operations.

Devine was happy to have five wise Preps accompanying him on the last difficult challenge. The elderly swifts from the Faithful church laid their wings on the five wise Preps, prayed for them, and then sent them on their way through the open door which mysteriously appeared before them in the bright morning sky.

11
Quackers

Devine led the five wise Preps high above the clouds. Penny admired the view as she turned and waved goodbye to her friends in Deli. Suddenly, as they soared forwards, she noticed that the fluffy white clouds in the sky were joining together like a white train behind them. The clouds then began to glow with a golden light because their edges were lined with gold. Glancing over their shoulders, with one eye watching where they were going, the other Preps checked out what Penny was getting so excited about.

"Wow, just look at the white and golden train," said Pablo, beginning to fly a bit too close to Pedro's tail.

"Watch out!" called Tiny Tim. But his squeaky voice couldn't be heard above the sound of the rushing winds.

It was too late. Pablo had collided with Pedro's bottom.

"Ouch, look where you're going!" shouted Pedro, feeling a bit sore.

Tiny Tim decided to fly up onto Pablo's long, strong back for the rest of the journey because he was only a little bird with a small pair of lungs and needed to catch his breath. Tiny Tim also thought it would be good to become an extra pair of eyes for the old eagle so that he wouldn't crash in mid-air again.

Devine had heard the hubbub and decided to speak to the Preps, sending messages to them on the secret winds that they needed to keep looking forwards.

"The next city we are going to is extremely odd. In fact it's quite quackers! Its full name is 'Laodicea' but our code name for it will be 'Od' City," whispered Devine.

"This sounds like it's going to be a real giggle," twittered Penny.

"Yes, the place will make you laugh because it's such a sham. Sadly, it's a comedy of errors," said Devine, not quite as amused as Penny, because the serious fact was that the church in Od City had been taken over by Pretenders. "Dr. Duck, the leader of the church in Od City, is a daft duck indeed. He tries to cover over his quirky, quacking ways by wearing a posh robe. Dr. Duck thinks that wearing the robe commands respect and makes him look superior. He's trying to fool all the church members into thinking that he's more important than them. In fact, he doesn't realise that he is actually naked!"

"Gasp!" went Oscar and Penny, taking in a couple of flies as they breathed in.

They began to cough and laugh at the same time at the thought of the naked duck. Pedro and Pablo just gave each other knowing glances because they had heard of this place before.

"I am gathering the gold-edged, white clouds and bringing them with me because the letter from Blazing Glory that I'm taking to the members of the Od church tells them to buy white clothes and gold to cover over their shame and poor behaviour. If they refuse, then all will be exposed when the Master returns," explained Devine.

Perched on Oscar's back, Penny read out loud to the wise Preps a copy of the letter being delivered from Blazing Glory to the Od church. It was a word-for-word copy of the following letter in the Bible:

Revelation chapter 3 verses 14 to 22

Rapidly, Devine began to descend over Od City. There was plenty of menacing mist around. Just ahead, there was a clearing and a very quaint-looking lily pond in the grounds of the church. The mist was taking its time to lift off the pond. One by one, the five wise Preps landed by Devine.

Who should be waddling around the grounds, with an air of importance, but Dr. Duck himself. He did look fine and dandy in his posh robe but the young Preps began to titter at the thought of him really being naked. Unaware of their smirking, Dr. Duck bowed in front of Devine.

"Duck!" cried out Pablo.

"I'm Dr. Duck, thank you," corrected the duck because he really liked his title and insisted that everyone show him respect by speaking to him properly.

"No, I mean 'duck'. . .!" replied Pablo.

But it was too late. Splat!

One of Vermont's buzzards was flying low over the lily pond and had dropped a dollop of pride right onto Dr. Duck's splendid robe. The stuff was white and runny and smelt very peculiar. Dr. Duck was furious and went round and round in circles going quackers. He then decided to wash off the pride splat in the lukewarm water in the lily pond. Ducks love lukewarm water. They don't like it hot or cold, just mild and lukewarm. This was a perfect opportunity for Devine to deliver his message to Dr. Duck so he got out the letter and read it to him.

"Father God demands that your love for him is either hot or cold," declared zealous Devine after finishing the letter, his eyes burning with fire from Blazing Glory. Then he added, "Lukewarm feelings make him feel sick."

The five wise Preps began to shake as the atmosphere around the lily pond changed. Dr. Duck dived into the water and buried his head in the mud at the bottom because he didn't want to listen to such negative news. He liked being lukewarm. It suited his feathers!

While Devine continued talking to Dr. Duck, the five wise Preps decided to go and find the Od church's robot. They knew that the wonky scenes they had just observed meant that the robot was faulty in some way. They wanted to examine it to find out exactly what the problems were that were affecting the church. They set off, hunting for clues.

It didn't take them long to discover a trail of puddles leading into the church and down one of the side aisles towards a heavy iron door. With a great long run-up and shove at the door, together the five Preps managed to force it open. Huffing and puffing, they tumbled and flapped down the stone steps that led into the basement. Water dripped down the steps and leaked from the pipes into the dark, damp underground room. Sure enough, they were right. Hidden in the shadows was the robot.

It was a very odd-looking robot. A bit of an ugly duckling really. Sadly, during the attack in Dry Valley one of its legs had been taken and this now affected its movement. The robot didn't like walking to the nearby  Olive Grove to fetch oil to oil its joints, so it had become very rusty. It had begun to behave like a wonky robot and this was affecting the behaviour of the Od church members in a negative way. Many of the members had allowed Pretenders to take control of operating the robot. Wonky robots are manipulative and always get their own way.

This fault was also reflected in Dr. Duck's unwillingness to change. Unfortunately, he had become very stuck in his ways. He wasn't moving backwards but neither was he moving forwards. He loved just spending time floating on his lukewarm lily pond. Of course, the church members just followed his example, and they too loved nothing better than spending all their time soaking in the lukewarm water.

As a result, the robot's other leg had become wrinkled, and because there wasn't much circulation in it, it was in danger of dropping off. This didn't help the rust problem either, and the rust was taking over the robot's entire body. If things weren't corrected soon, then the robot would be unable to walk. If that happened, the effects on the church members would be life-threatening and the Od church would have to close.

The five wise Preps decided to head back up the stairs and take a look inside the church to see how the members had been affected by the robot's condition but the heavy door had slammed shut behind them and they couldn't get out. They knocked and knocked again but no-one answered. They waited and waited like patient Preps. Penny and the others flew up to peer out through a rectangular-shaped opening at the top of the door.

"Hello, is anyone there?" piped up little Penny shouting through the flap, but there was no answer. The persevering sparrow didn't give up hope and called through the flap again. "Cooee!" she shrieked.

Finally, they caught sight of the ducks and geese who were the church members. They were obviously Pretenders because they were very free and easy in their behaviour and attitudes. The Master had given them freedom, but they had taken it and used it in the wrong way. Instead of being free to please Father God, they were now freely pleasing themselves.

The geese were the main problem because instead of attending to their duties they were gandering around, causing mischief. Ms. Quackers was in charge of the geese but she was too busy quacking around as a busy body. The older busy-body geese had forgotten how to teach and train the young geese to behave properly. Sadly, the young geese liked to bully the little ducklings and had formed their own gang. No ugly ducklings were allowed in their elite group. Bully Bear had influenced the nasty geese into becoming Pretenders while he spent time lurking in the woods in the grounds of the church building.

With no reply the Preps, who were beginning to feel scared that they were stuck in the basement, decided that they would have to try and force open the heavy iron door again. It was harder to do this from the inside because it was so dark, and they had to take a running leap up the stairs which were slippery from all the dripping water. After five attempts, they managed to push open the door and then had to spend a few moments brushing down their wet feathers and getting their breath back.

Heading back out of the church, the five Preps used their magnifying glasses to go in search of Pretenders. They followed a trail of webbed prints which had been left in the mud around the lily pond and then flew close to the ground, through a pretty bluebell wood. Penny asked the others to stop so that she could admire the lovely blue flowers.

"Hey, chaps, can we stop here for a short while? The bluebells remind me of my grandmother!" shouted Penny as loudly as she could.

All the boys landed in a bit of a huff as they wanted adventure and not a walk on a pretty nature trail. They stared at Penny with an impatient glare. Suddenly, they heard the roar of a bear raging through the trees.

"That sounds like Bully Bear!" cried Oscar in a flap.

The five wise Preps were not going to hang around to find out if it was him or not. With great speed, they did an emergency take-off. They flew through a clearing in the woods and at last they found the geese gathered in a small park called Liberty Place. Out of breath, they landed near a huge duck pond where all the ducks and geese loved to chill out.

The pond in Liberty Place was bigger and better than the pond at the Od church. Slowly, the young geese were exploring how geese in a bigger pond live and play. It was a beautiful evening and the sun had begun to set in a blaze of warm, red colour.

Ms. Quackers, Dr. Duck's close friend, was being a busy body, asking everyone's opinion about the red evening sky in the distance. She loved to show off her intelligence which was a degree above everyone elses.

"What do you think the red sky might be saying to us?" asked Ms. Quackers.

"Red sky at night, shepherd's delight!" cried out one smart goose.

"Red sky in the morning means the shepherd's house is on fire," laughed Lucy goosy gander, a rebellious little lady. Lucy goosy gander was Ms. Quackers' daughter and she showed her mother no respect at all.

Penny wondered why they were so busy looking for a sign but ignoring and disobeying the simple words they could find in their Bibles. With the bad attitudes being shown by the geese, Tiny Tim got out his Bible and read out the words Jesus the Master had spoken when he had addressed a similar problem:

Matthew chapter 12 verses 38 to 42

The nosey geese overheard what Tiny Tim had just read and were furious at his comments. The young geese never read their own Bibles, so they didn't realise that these were words spoken by the Master, Jesus. They ganged up like a gaggle and began to chase the five wise Preps from Liberty Place and back to the lily pond at the Od church.

"Quack, quack, quack, quackers!" roared the gaggle of geese.

"Quick, quick, quick, quicker!" replied old Pablo, trying to keep up with the other four wise Preps.

The gaggling geese were unashamed of being Pretenders. They behaved one way when they were inside the church and another way when they were outside the building. Once the five Preps were back at the lily pond, the geese gave up the chase and pretended they were just rushing back to the Od church.

Relieved, the five wise Preps sat by the lukewarm lily pond. They breathed in heavily, trying to calm their fears. While they waited for Devine to finish talking with Dr. Duck, Oscar couldn't help wondering what the disgusting smell was, wafting through the air. He sniffed and then sniffed again. Phew! He knew it couldn't be Tiny Tim because the smell was too big and bad to be coming from him. So he questioned Pedro and Pablo instead, to see if they were responsible for the bad stink.

"It's not me," responded Pedro.

"Well, don't blame me!" reacted Pablo.

They were off again. Pedro flew away and so did Pablo. The smelly mist seemed to be taking its toll on the five wise Preps.

Devine noticed what was happening and cried out, "Come back Pedro, and come back Pablo!"

They quickly obeyed. Devine went on to explain that the smell was due to the dirty water in the pond. As the water didn't flow or move and was just lukewarm, it had become stagnant. This was the bad smell and because of this there was no life in the pond either.

"No life?" said Pedro. "How can I do any fishing?"

The smell and the mist, as well as the low-flying buzzards, were making the place just too dangerous to be in, so Devine decided to take the five wise Preps to an  Olive Grove just on the edge of Od City. They tried to find Dr. Duck, to say goodbye to him, but he had buried his head again in the mud in the lily pond and was too embarrassed to look up.

Devine took off and as he flew he dragged the gold-edged

white clouds across the red sky. He sent out a message on the secret winds, calling for any birds that wanted to listen to the Master to come and buy white clothes and gold so they could be ready for Jesus's return. Even though Dr. Duck had rejected the letter from Blazing Glory, Devine still wanted to give the other church members at Od the opportunity to hear and respond to Father God's message. The Preps at the Od church were being separated from the Pretenders, ready for the Last Hour.

The vivid picture of the train of white and gold clouds rushing through the sky sent out a sign to all in Od City. Many of the birds didn't like this sign because they realised it meant they needed to repent, which means to say sorry and turn away from wrong ways. Happily, there was a small group that did respond and they flew without hesitation into the Olive Grove.

Pedro looked at the growing crowd but he wasn't very impressed because a large number of the birds were pigeons. Pigeons often carry diseases due to the unclean places they like to visit.

Pedro was about to begin speaking, but before he had a chance to open his beak, the crowd all looked upwards and saw the gold-edged white clouds joining together and coming down from the skies like a large bright-white sheet. Tiny crystal droplets dripped from the giant sheet and splashed into the eyes of the watching birds. They all had eye infections caused by the effects of the menacing mist and the lukewarm water. The healing droplets removed the infections so that every bird could see clearly once again. On the sheet was every species of bird you could imagine.

A feather, carrying a special message for Pedro to read out

loud to those gathered in the Olive Grove, wafted down from the sheet.

Acts chapter 10

It was a long read but the clear message of it was that Blazing Glory was open to all. The colour of their feathers or where they had come from was not important to Father God. Jesus was standing, knocking at the door. He was waiting to come but first he called for everyone to be ready before his sudden return. Pedro explained this tale. He wanted everyone to share the great big offer of love being given to those who would receive Jesus, the Master.

They all then soaked themselves in oil as they prayed, and the poor, naked birds bought the white cloth and gold. Instead of paying with money, they were asked to swap their old cloaks, which covered up their shameful ways, and were each given a bright-white clean robe, edged with gold, by the Master.

"You are to say 'yes' and do everything the Master asks you to do, and to say 'no' to everything that the Master does not want you to do," warned Devine. "Anything else is from the evil genius."

Pablo opened the pages of his Bible and looked through his magnifying glass to find a special verse to read to the listening birds. These words showed them how important it was, in order to be a good Prep, to keep their promise to Jesus, the Master.

Matthew chapter 5 verse 37

The pigeons responded quickly to Devine's call and moved towards him, nodding their heads. Amazingly, their ugly grey feathers were transformed into brilliant white so that they became like pure white doves. Their wing-tips were miraculously edged with gold. They were now ready for the huge feast being prepared in Blazing Glory. Only those wearing the special feast garments would be allowed in.

Tiny Tim was very skilled in knowing where everything was found in the Bible, so he quickly searched with his magnifying glass to find the reference to this dress code.

Matthew chapter 22 verses 1 to 14

To Devine's delight, everyone in the Olive Grove had now received their fresh oil and had the right robes on, ready for the Master's return. The five wise Preps were glad they had been able to help Devine succeed with this mission.

Due to the heavy, dark mist beginning to rise from all the duck ponds in the area, Devine decided they would rest in the Olive Grove for the night. He seemed a little restless as the five wise Preps settled into their nests in the olive trees, and he kept reminding them that the hour was late and it wouldn't be long before the Master returned. Pablo tried to sleep with one eye open as he knew that Jesus's return, also called 'the second coming', would happen in a twinkling moment. Devine smiled at his enthusiasm and then gently closed his eyelid with a brush from his wing.

Devine flew into the night sky and circled the Od City church. He kept on tapping on the door but no-one opened it, so he pushed the letter from Blazing Glory through the letterbox. As he did so, he prayed, hoping the church members would answer the call to change their pretending ways.

12
Coming, Ready or Not?

The night passed quickly and the five wise Preps were woken with an urgent morning call from Devine. While the birds got ready and washed their feathers, preening them into place, Devine lost himself in his thoughts. He was troubled by the changing morning skies. The broken clouds were beginning to glow a deep-red colour.

"Hurry, hurry, time is short!" cried Devine.

Quickly, they all left their nests to follow Devine who had taken off at a rapid pace. All that could be seen across the ground was the ever-increasing menacing mist. Even the five wise Preps began to yawn as the poisonous mist tried to put them to sleep. Devine called them to fly higher up so they wouldn't be affected by it as it rose from the ground.

They flew in silence for almost three hours. Penny broke the silence when she saw Dry Valley in the distance. "What's going on in Dry Valley?" she called out.

A lot of flight activity was taking place. Lots of Preps were battling with Vermont's cruel buzzard army. These Preps were impressive freedom flyers who had mastered flying above the mist.

As Penny and her friends scanned the valley, they noticed

that it was filling up with water. Some birds were paddling on the edge of the water but they were finding the tide too deep so they were taking off for higher ground.

The five wise Preps followed Devine under the cover of his light, which kept them safe from the lurking buzzards. Devine flew straight ahead to the huge  Olive Grove at the base of Mount Olivet. One by one, the birds landed on a high tree top which gave them a magnificent view of the valley.

There had not been a day like this in history before. What they were watching was a great battle between the oncoming mist which was poisonous and destructive, and the river which teemed with life and power. While the mist was being poured into the valley by Vermont, the strong tide of the roaring river pushed it back again. It seemed as if Vermont was making one big last effort to cover the earth with his evil mist. At the same time, Father God was making one last loving effort to save those who would follow the way to Blazing Glory before Jesus's return.

Once they were safe and sound, with their tube pots full of oil from the dripping olive trees, Devine said a fond farewell to the five wise Preps.

"Well done, my friends, you have been good and loyal servants. Now I have to return to Blazing Glory for an urgent meeting. It's very important that you stay here watching and waiting because the Master, Jesus is coming very soon. Do not go to sleep," warned the masterful Devine. "I'm only a prayer away, so don't be afraid."

One at a time, he encouraged each of the five wise Preps before taking off into the flaming red sky. As he flew, the sky opened up with a beam of light. It was just like a door had opened in heaven and then quickly closed again. The Preps were stunned for a moment and sat quietly watching the view.

Young Penny became a little restless at this point because the ever-approaching mist was affecting her mood. Oscar tried to encourage her by reminding her of the eight Be-attitude stripes which should by now be colouring her wings. The older wise Preps already had their stripes firmly sewn onto their wing feathers. They had earned their stripes through all the trouble and testing they had gone through in their service for the Master.

Tiny Tim calmed Penny down as he rubbed some of the blue dye from his chest onto her wing. After a few gentle rubs, the blue dye began to highlight the special stripes that had begun to form on her brown feathers. Penny felt so encouraged because she loved wearing bright colours. She was now the proud owner of eight Be-attitude blue stripes, along with her 12 fruit badges from the *Trick or Treat?* adventure, and she sat there admiring them all.

Meanwhile, Pablo the bald eagle couldn't stop peering at Dry Valley. He suddenly remembered a chapter in the Bible which would help the Preps to understand what was happening in Dry Valley. Excitedly, using their magnifying glasses, they searched for it together.

Ezekiel chapter 47 verses 1 to 12

While Pablo used his great knowledge to help teach his younger friends, Pedro seized the opportunity to go fishing in the teeming river. He couldn't help it because he was the great kingfisher. He wasn't the kind of bird to miss such a great opportunity, even in such perilous times. Pedro caught more fish on that one day than he had done in his whole lifetime. He managed to help and reach many that were lost and needed rescuing with the Good News about Jesus. When he returned from his fishing trip, Pedro and the other watching birds were exhausted.

They nested on the highest tree top in the Olive Grove but such were the efforts of Vermont that the mist was even able to get to where they were perched. Vermont was bubbling with fiery anger because he knew his time was nearly up. He had been warned of the severe judgement coming to him from Blazing Glory. He was responsible for the tragic destruction being seen on the earth, so he and his followers deserved the worst punishment possible.

Gradually, the five wise Preps drifted off into a light sleep. How long they slept for, they were unable to tell. After a short time, feathers carrying the words from a psalm drifted like a blanket of snow onto the top of their nest.

Psalm 32 verses 6 & 7

One of the feathers tickled Pablo's nose, which made him snore. The sudden noise woke the other Preps from their sleep.

"How long were we asleep for?" asked Penny, stretching and rubbing her tiny sparrow eyes with her wings.

"I'm not sure," said Oscar, straightening up his glasses.

They read the words from the feathers and then dropped them in fright as a loud trumpet-like sound rang around Mount Olivet. The ground began to shake and then shake some more.

"What's happening?" cried Penny very alarmed, clinging on to Oscar. "Aghhh!"

"Keep watching!" ordered Pablo, trying to be big and brave.

Rocks then began to dislodge and roll down the side of the mountain, crashing into the river of rapids running through Dry Valley. Strangely enough, the buzzards were nowhere to be seen. It seemed as if they were hiding.

Everywhere was very dark, so the five wise Preps lit the oil in their tube pots to give them some light. Pedro began singing 'This little light of mine, I'm going to let it shine' in an effort to make the lamps on their wings burn brighter.

"What's happening?" asked the question-master, Penny.

Tiny Tim took hold of his magnifying glass and read Penny a story that Jesus had told, to help comfort her at this difficult time.

Matthew chapter 25 verses 1 to 13

Just as Tiny Tim finished this exciting story, five well-known birds flew up onto the branch next to them in the olive tree. Who should it be but Priscilla the peacock, Nikey Nick the rooster, Bella the sparrowhawk, Chip the woodpecker and, with a grand entrance and still wearing his pride-splattered robe, Dr. Duck.

Frantically, the five birds begged for some oil from the five wise Preps. Unfortunately, there had been a flood in the Olive Groves and so there was no more oil around. The five foolish birds hadn't paid any of the Olive Groves a visit in a very long time, so their tube pots were bone dry. Unusually, Devine couldn't help them either because he had been summoned to Blazing Glory.

"Why have you been so foolish and not listened to the warnings?" asked the wise bald eagle Pablo. "You can't have any of our oil because we won't have enough for ourselves, so you must go and see if you can buy some in the city below."

There was no time to lose. As soon as Pablo had finished speaking, the shrill sound of a trumpet could be heard. It was such a piercing noise that no-one's voice could be heard any more.

The five foolish Pretenders flew off rapidly to try and find some oil to buy. Dr. Duck got his robe caught in the branches of the trees as he tried to keep up with the other fools. The branches pulled the cloak clean off his back and revealed to the watching crowd his naked, ugly brown feathers. Trying to keep his dignity intact he flew on as if nothing had happened. His pride had resulted in his spectacular fall.

"He looks quackers!" agreed all five wise Preps as they followed the trumpet call to the summit of Mount Olivet.

"Pride always comes before a fall," remarked knowing Pablo.

With one final blast there was a flash of light which twinkled like a blaze in the sky and then there was a sudden eerie silence. With the silence came an unexpected terror. A great panic was felt around the earth and the five foolish Pretenders rushed back to the great mountain, Mount Olivet. They were sure this would be the place the Master would return to as it was the mountain from where he had left the earth to go back to Blazing Glory.

"Jesus is coming back to the same place and in the same way he left," quacked Dr. Duck desperately as he waddled around in a state of panic.

However, to their dismay, there was no sign of Jesus or the five wise Preps. In fact, there was not a single Prep left anywhere on the planet. It seemed that the Master had come like a thief in the night. This truly was a day like no other.

"Jesus came back and we weren't ready!" cried Prickly Priscilla, trying not to dampen her feathers with the rush of tears falling off her beak.

Dr. Duck had a moment of inspiration when he found a magnifying glass and Bible which had been left by a disappearing Prep. He looked up the last verses in the Bible and read them out loud to the others. They were desperately hoping to find out how everything would end.

Revelation chapter 22 verses 20 & 21

"You really are quackers if you think we have been mistaken. This is a terrible day!" cried Prickly Priscilla. Her great colourful feathers were of no importance now.

Nikey Nick looked down at his gold Rolex watch. It seemed as if time had stood still. A teardrop rolled down off his beak and splashed onto his fancy tick-tock. "There's no time left and we have been left behind!" crowed the devastated rooster.

Chip gave his final tap with his beak onto the bark on the tree trunk and sadly got it stuck. His head was held down in despair as the five fools stood still.

What happened to the Preps and what will happen to the Pretenders who are left behind is a tale for another day. Watch, wait and be ready because this great new day is about to dawn. It will be a happy day for those who are prepared and watching for the Master's return but a sad and terrible one for those who are not ready for the hour.

www.blazing-glory.com

Hi there!

We hope you have enjoyed reading *The Pretenders*. It is the second book in a three-part series called 'Blazing Glory', beginning with the book *Trick or Treat?* and there will be a final story out in the not-too-distant future.

If you want to know even more about Blazing Glory and follow new adventures every week, then go to the Blazing Glory website, www.blazing-glory.com.

Meet all the characters and enjoy new journeys on the way to Blazing Glory as you discover words of wisdom and stories of faith, courage, hope and love.

Many of you will want to start out on your own journey of adventure to Blazing Glory. Every week you can find help on your journey on the Blazing Glory website. But never forget that all the help you need is in your manual (Bible) and time spent in your Olive Grove, and that your helper, Jesus, is just a prayer away.

If you do not already know God as your Father and Jesus as your friend, and you would like to, then why not go to your special Olive Grove and pray the following short prayer:

'Father, please forgive me for the times I have not been

true to you and what you say. I am sorry for all the wrong things I have done, and from today I want to be free to live in your truth. I thank you, Jesus, that you paid the price for each one of my sins and I receive the forgiveness found at the cross. I receive you – the truth – into my heart and I know that through you I now have eternal life. I pray that your Holy Spirit will live in me and guide me in your way. Amen.'

Jesus has now come into your heart and he promises never to leave you if you follow his ways. If you want to, you could tell a good friend, family member or adult whom you trust that you have just done this. Or you could tell the Blazing Glory team by sending an email to us at info@blazing-glory.com